Approach for Windows™ 95

by Shelley O'Hara

A Division of Macmillan Computer Publishing USA
201 West 103rd St., Indianapolis, Indiana 46290

International Standard Book Number: 0-7897-0647-4

Library of Congress Catalog Card Number: 95-71450

97 96 95 8 7 6 5 4 3 2 1

Interpretation of the printing code: the rightmost number of the first series of numbers is the year of the book's printing; the rightmost number of the second series of numbers is the number of the book's printing. For example, a printing code of 95-1 shows that the first printing of the book occurred in 1995.

Printed in the United States of America

Publisher: Roland Elgey
Vice President and Publisher: Marie Butler-Knight
Editorial Services Director: Elizabeth Keaffaber
Publishing Manager: Barry Pruett
Managing Editor: Michael Cunningham
Development Editor: David Bradford
Production Editor: Paige Widder
Cover Designer: Dan Armstrong
Designer: Barb Kordesh
Technical Specialist: Cari Skaggs
Indexer: Mary Jane Frisby
Production: Jason Carr, Bryan Flores, DiMonique Ford, Bob LaRoche, Julie Quinn, Scott Tullis, Jody York, Karen York

Acknowledgments

Special thanks to the many editors that worked on this book: Martha O'Sullivan, for inviting me to do this project; David Bradford, for making suggestions on the content and organization; Richard Eisenmenger, for checking the book for technical accuracy; and last but not least, Paige Widder, for editing and handling the book through production.

Trademarks

Contents

Introduction

It used to be that database programs were huge, complex programs designed to be used mostly by computer programmers. If you wanted to set up and use a database, you had to pretty much master another language—a database programming language.

In recent years, databases have gotten somewhat more approachable. In fact, Approach is one of the most highly recommended database programs for beginning users. Approach is simple; the program is designed to make it easy to set up and use a database. But do not be fooled; although Approach is simple, it's still a powerful tool. Approach is also a full-featured relational database program with features for joining databases, creating macros, and more. You can use the program to do as much or as little as you want.

You can use Approach for business purposes (to track clients, orders, inventory, invoices, employees), personal purposes (track friends, wine lists, music collections, books), or both. You can create data entry forms, reports, worksheets, charts, and more.

To take advantage of all these program features, you just need to get started. But how do you do that?

Get Started With This Book

This book makes it as easy as 1-2-3 to get started with Approach.

First, rather than overwhelm you with lots of details at once, this book breaks topics into manageable chunks. The book focuses on the features you are most likely to need and to use; you don't have to learn each and every feature.

Understanding Approach Databases

In this lesson, you will learn what a database is and how it is set up. This lesson provides the background information you need to know in order to use Approach.

What Is a Database?

A *database* is basically a collection of related information. For example, you might have a database to keep track of your CD collection. Or if you have a business, you might have a database of your clients or your inventory. The entire collection of information is the database, and that database is structured into fields and records.

A *field* is one piece of information. For example, in a database of your clients, you may have fields for last name, first name, company name, address, city, state, ZIP, phone, and so on. Each of these pieces of information would be stored in a field with a field name that identified the information.

A *record* is one set of information or set of fields. In the client database, for instance, you would have a record for each client, and that record would consist of that person's specific name, address, and so on.

What Is a View?

If a database were just a list of fields, you would be fairly limited in what you could do. Instead, the main purpose for creating and working in a database is to have the flexibility to manipulate that data. You can view just some fields—for example, make a phone list from Last Name, First name, and Phone Number fields, leaving out the addresses. Or you can view fields from more than one database—for example, combining address fields from a customer database and stock numbers from an inventory database to create an order form.

In Approach, you can work with the data in different ways. You can use a form to enter data, or create a report to summarize data. Each of these is a different type of view. You can create and work in the following types of views:

- **Forms** A form shows data one record at a time and is useful for entering and reviewing the individual records in a database. Lesson 6 covers using a form to enter records; Lessons 15–18 cover creating and modifying forms.
- **Reports** In a report, you can display several records on a page. You can also summarize and perform calculations on the data. For more data on creating, formatting, and printing reports, review Lessons 19–21.
- **Form Letters** Many databases are used to store information (names and addresses) about people. Often you want to use that list of information to do a mailing. For example, you may want to do a mailing announcing a new service. When you want to send the same information to several people, you can create a form letter. Lesson 22 explains how to create form letters.
- **Mailing Labels** If you do a mailing, you won't want to have to address the envelopes by hand. Instead, you can use Approach to create mailing labels and/or envelopes for you. Check out Lesson 23 for complete information on mailing labels.
- **Worksheets** If you have used a spreadsheet program, such as Excel, you are probably familiar with worksheets. A worksheet presents data in a column-and-row structure. This type of view is covered in Lesson 24.

- **Charts** A chart is another way to visually summarize the data in your worksheet. Charts are covered in Lesson 26.
- **Crosstabs** A crosstab is a special type of worksheet that enables you to categorize and summarize information in the worksheet. (See Lesson 25.)

When you create a new database, Approach sets up two default views: a form and a worksheet. You can then add any other types of views you want to work with to the database.

What Is an Approach Database?

Now that you understand how a database is structured and the different ways you can work within that structure, you need to understand how Approach handles the actual files. When you set up a database in Approach, you basically have two types of files: The Approach file stores all of the different views you create. For example, if you create a form, report, form letters, and mailing labels, they are stored in the Approach file. (All the views are stored together in one file.) Approach files use the extension APR.

The database file stores the data you use to create the different views. You can think of this file as the behind-the-scenes file; you don't really work with this file. Instead, you work with the data through the views. The database file can be stored in one of several different file formats (each with a different extension). For example, you can open or save a dBASE file (DBF file).

Planning a Database

Once you are ready to create your own database, you should spend some time planning the structure of the database before you get started. Doing so will make sure the database contains all the information you need in the order you want.

What Is the Purpose?

The first step in creating a new database is to describe or define the purpose of the database. What do you hope to gain by creating the database? What is the goal? Think about what you want to get from the data. Do you want to track sales by sales reps? Do you want to send mailings to clients? Once you understand what you want to do, you can more clearly set up the database to accomplish this goal.

What Data Do You Need?

After you know the goal or purpose of the database, your next step is to make a list of the information you need to include. What do you have to enter to get to your goal? Think about how you will find and sort the data and be sure to include separate fields for each piece of information.

For example, if you wanted to set up a database for your clients, you may want to include the following fields: Last Name, First Name, Company Name, Address, City, State, ZIP, Phone. You may also want to include other information, such as a customer number, or the sales rep assigned to this client.

Notice that each field has a unique name and that each piece of information is in a separate field. For example, you could put the first and last name together, but doing so may prevent you from sorting the clients by last name. The same is true for city and state.

In Approach, you can work with more than one database at a time, so you don't have to lump all the information you need into one database file. In fact, you might—and should—divide the information into separate databases. For example, rather than track orders in your client database, you can create a separate database for orders and then join the two when you need to display or report data from both files.

Draw it! You may want to sketch out the databases you need on paper. Make a list of the fields you need. You can also draw the relationships between various databases, if you are setting up more than one.

WHICH METHOD SHOULD YOU USE?

After you understand the purpose and have a pretty clear idea of the structure of the database, you can decide which is the best method to create your database. In Approach, you can use one of two methods. You can create a database from scratch or you can use a SmartMaster.

Approach provides several predefined databases, called SmartMasters. These databases are set up and ready to use; you simply select the one you want. (See Lesson 4 for information on using a SmartMaster.) You can pretty much tell the purpose of the SmartMaster by its name: Accounts, Authors, Collection, Contacts, Employees, Events, Expenses, Inventory, Membership List, Suppliers, and Video Library.

Using one of the SmartMasters lets you get started quickly because you don't have to set up the fields yourself. If one of the SmartMasters comes close to what you want, consider using this method. Keep in mind that you can modify the database structure—add fields, change fields, delete fields. So you can always start with a SmartMaster and then modify it so that the structure meets your needs.

If none of the SmartMasters suits your needs or if you don't want to try that method, you can also create a database from scratch. Setting up a database using this method is the topic of Lesson 5.

In this lesson, you learned some of the underlying database concepts that you need to understand before you get started creating a new database. The next lesson explains how to start Approach and how to exit Approach.

Getting Started

In this lesson, you will learn how to start Approach, you'll take a look at the Approach screen, select a menu command, and exit.

Starting Approach

Before you can start Approach, you must do two things. The first is to install the program. You can find brief installation instructions on the inside front cover of this book.

Windows 95 starts automatically each time you turn on your computer, so if your computer is on, you should see the Windows desktop. At the bottom left corner you should see a Start button, which you use to start programs.

To start Approach, follow these steps:

1. Click the Start button to display the Start menu.
2. Move the pointer onto the Programs command. You see a list of program folders and some program icons. The list will vary depending on how you have set up your programs.
3. Move the pointer onto the program folder that contains Approach until you see the Approach icon (see Figure 2.1). The series of folders you select will depend on which folder you placed the program in when you installed the program.

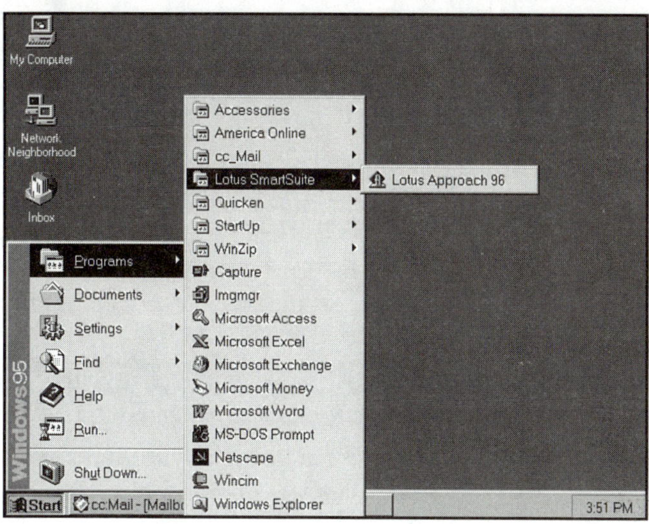

FIGURE 2.1 The Approach program icon.

4. When you see the Approach program icon, click on it. The program is started.

Can't find the program icon? Look for a folder called Lotus Applications, or through other folders until you find the Approach icon.

UNDERSTANDING THE APPROACH SCREEN

When you start Approach, you are prompted to open an existing database or create a new one. These topics are covered later in the book. After you select a database option, you see the Approach program window, which includes tools for working with the database (see Figure 2.2). Notice the different on-screen elements that help you use the program:

ELEMENT	DESCRIPTION
Menu bar	Use the menu bar to select commands, as covered in the next section.
Icon bar	This bar includes a row of buttons called SmartIcons. You can use these buttons to access frequently used commands.
Action bar	Use this bar to perform key database actions, such as creating a new record or searching for records.
View tabs	These tabs enable you to change the view of the database. Views are explained in Lesson 4.
Status bar	The status bar gives you information about the current database (for example, the current record number). You can also use the buttons on the status bar to display pop-up menus.

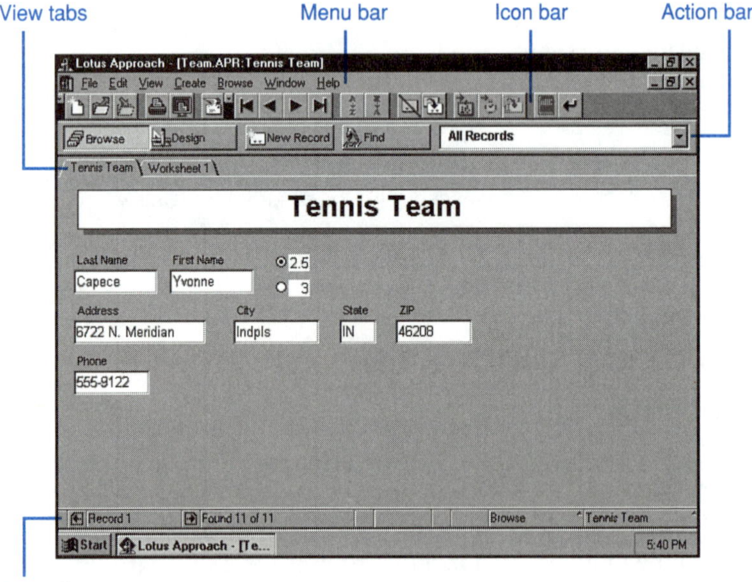

FIGURE 2.2 The Approach screen.

The Approach screen also includes standard Windows controls for resizing and closing the window.

SELECTING A MENU COMMAND

When you want to do something in the database—for example, sort the records—you issue a command. The easiest way to select a command is to use the mouse:

1. Click on the menu name. You see a drop-down list of commands.
2. Click on the command you want.
3. Depending on the command you selected, one of the following occurs:
    - If the command is followed by an arrow, you see a submenu of commands. Click on the command you want from this menu.
    - If the command is followed by an ellipses, you see a dialog box (see Figure 2.3). Make your selections in the dialog box and click OK to confirm the command or Cancel to close the dialog box without executing the command.

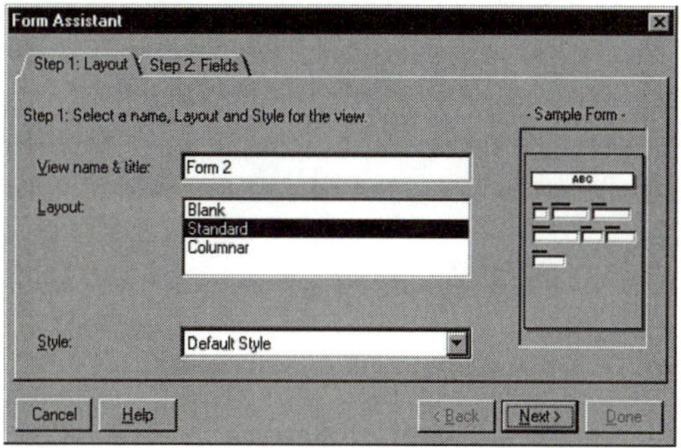

FIGURE 2.3 When you select some commands, you see a dialog box.

In some cases, the command is executed immediately after you choose it. You don't need to do anything else.

Prefer the keyboard? If you prefer to keep your hands on the keyboard, you can use it to select commands. You can use keyboard shortcuts (noted on the menu) or you can use the keyboard to open and select commands. Press Alt+*letter* (where *letter* is the underlined character within the menu choice) to display the menu. Press the key letter of the menu (again the underlined letter) to select the command you want.

USING THE ICON, ACTION, AND STATUS BAR

As mentioned, the icon, action, and status bar provide a quick method of executing different database options. For example, the icon bar includes SmartIcons for opening a file, sorting the database, inserting the date, and more. The action bar includes buttons for changing to design view, adding a new record, and so on. (See the inside back cover for a reference list of the default icon bar and action bar icons.)

SmartIcon A palette of buttons, each representing a certain command. As a shortcut, you can use the SmartIcon rather than the menu command to perform the task.

To use an icon, simply click on it. If you aren't sure what an icon does, you can display a balloon description by pointing to the icon with the mouse pointer and clicking the right mouse button.

The status bar not only includes information about the database, but also provides access to pop-up menus for changing the view, moving among the records, and so on. To display a pop-up menu, click on that area in the status bar. For example, to change to a different view, click on the area that lists the current view. Then select the view you want from the pop-up menu.

EXITING APPROACH

When you are finished working in Approach, you can exit the program. Approach will prompt you to save any work that has not been saved. If you have added new records, Approach saves them automatically. When you are designing new views (such as creating a new form), don't forget to save your work.

Follow these steps to exit Approach:

1. Open the File menu and select the Exit command.
2. If prompted to save your work, choose Yes to save, No to cancel.

Shortcut! You can also press Alt+F4 to exit Approach. Or click the Close button in the program window.

In this lesson, you learned how to start Approach and take a look at some of the on-screen elements that will help you as you use the program. In the next lesson, you will learn how to use the help utilities that come with Approach.

Getting Help

In this lesson, you will learn how to use the online help system to get help.

Using Help Contents

Most programs include many, many features and commands, and Approach is no exception. Remembering how to use it all seems impossible. Rather than memorize each feature, you can use the help system when you want a reminder of what a feature does or when you can't remember how to perform a certain task.

Approach provides several different methods for getting help: you can select a topic from a table of contents, look up a topic in the index, or search for a particular topic.

To look up a topic in the help contents, follow these steps:

1. Open the Help menu and select the Help Topics command.
2. If necessary, click the Contents tab. You see a list of topics, indicated with a book icon.
3. Double-click on the book icon for the topic you want. Do this until you see topics indicated with a question mark icon; these are the topics for which you can display help (see Figure 3.1).

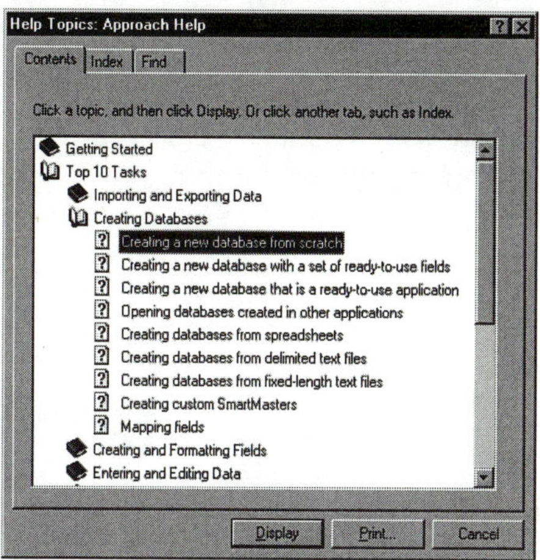

FIGURE 3.1 Select the topic you want.

4. Double-click on a topic with a question mark icon to display a help window (see Figure 3.2).

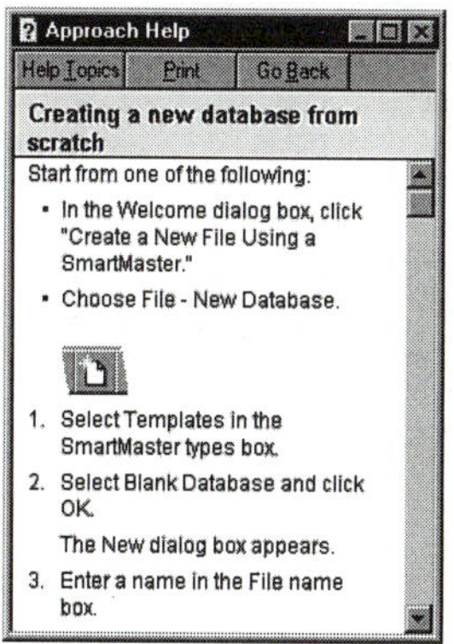

FIGURE 3.2 Use the help window to review information about a particular topic.

5. When you are finished reviewing the information, click the Close button.

USING HELP INDEX

In addition to using the Contents tab to look up a topic, you can look up a topic with the Index tab. To do this, you type the first few letters of the topic you want to find; then Approach displays any matching topics. You can select the one you want. Follow these steps:

1. Open the Help menu and select the Help Topics command.
2. Click the Index tab. You see Index tab shown in Figure 3.3.

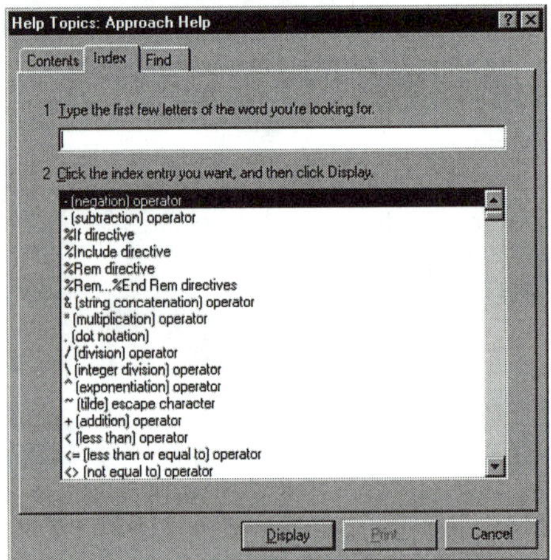

FIGURE 3.3 The Index tab.

3. Type the beginning letter(s) of the topic. As you do this, Help moves down the list to the items that match (see Figure 3.4).
4. Select the topic you want from the list.

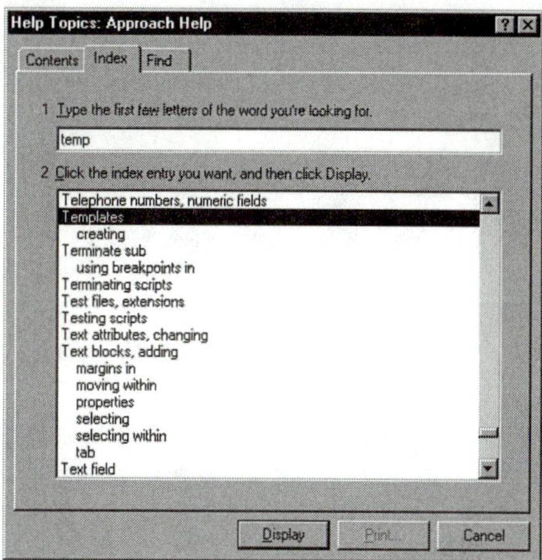

FIGURE 3.4 Approach displays matching topics.

SEARCHING FOR A TOPIC

If you can't find the topic in the contents screen or in the index, you can try searching for the topic with the Find tab. Approach will display any topics that include the word or words you type. Follow these steps to search for a topic:

1. Open the Help menu and select the Help Topics command.
2. Click the Find tab. (The first time you use this feature, you have to set up the files. Follow the on-screen instructions.)
3. Type the topic you want to find. As you do this, Approach displays matching topics in the middle of the dialog box (see Figure 3.5).

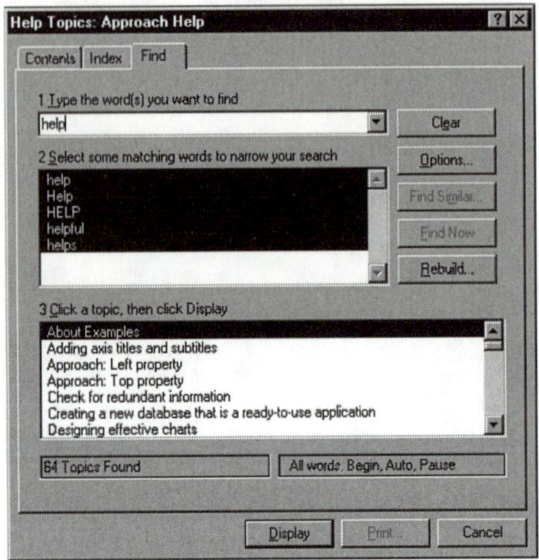

FIGURE 3.5 Approach searches the word list and displays matching topics.

4. Select matching topics in the middle area of the dialog box to narrow the search.
5. Double-click the topic to look up in the bottom area of the dialog box. Approach displays help information.

Dialog box help To get help about a dialog box option, click on the question mark button in the title bar of the dialog box. Then click on the option for which you want help. You see a short explanation of the option.

In this lesson, you learned how to use the help that comes with Approach. In the next lesson, you will learn how to create a new database with a SmartMaster.

LESSON 4

Creating a New Database from a SmartMaster

In this lesson, you will learn how to create a new database using one of the predefined databases, called SmartMasters.

Selecting the SmartMaster

To make it as easy as possible to set up a new database, Approach includes over 50 predesigned databases. These databases are set up for specific purposes, ranging from invoices to wine lists, from guest lists to stocks and bonds. Each database includes several fields suitable for the purpose. For example, if you use the membership list SmartMaster, you'll find fields for the name and address of the member as well as fields for date joined, dues, dues paid, and so on.

Using a SmartMaster template helps you get started quickly because you don't have to build all the fields yourself. If there's a SmartMaster that's close to what you need, check it out before you build a database from scratch. You can use the database as is, or you can modify the fields so that the database is more suited toward your needs.

Follow these steps:

1. When you start Approach, you see the Welcome to Lotus Approach dialog box. You can create a file from this dialog box by clicking on the Create a New File Using a SmartMaster tab (see Figure 4.1). Or you can open the File menu and select the New Database command.

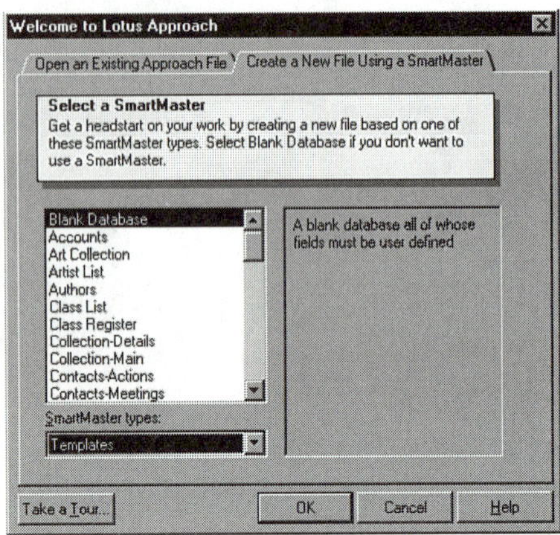

FIGURE 4.1 Select the SmartMaster you want to use.

2. Display the SmartMaster types drop-down list and select Templates. Approach displays a list of the available templates.
3. To see a short description of a SmartMaster, click on it. In the right half of the dialog box, Approach displays a description. You can use this description to find the file you want.
4. After you select the SmartMaster, click OK.

After selecting the SmartMaster, you must name the database and select a folder for it. The next section covers these tasks.

NAMING THE DATABASE

Remember that an Approach database consists of two files: the Approach file, which saves all the different views, and the database file, which contains the data. The first time you create a new database, you are prompted to assign a name and location (folder) for the new database file. For the name, you can type up to 255 characters. (Longer file names are one of the new features of

Windows 95.) You can include spaces, but you cannot include the following characters:

\ / < > * " | : ; ?

Approach will suggest a name that is basically a shortened version of the SmartMaster. You can use this name or type a different one. It's a good idea to use a descriptive name that will remind you of the purpose of the database.

In addition to typing a name, you can select a folder in which to place your new database. By default, Approach selects the Approach folder, but you may want to create a new folder to keep your databases stored separately from the program files.

Finally, you can select a file format for the database file. The default is dBASE IV (DBF), but you can select FoxPro, Paradox, Oracle, or other file types. The type of file you create will affect your options for setting up fields in the database. For example, dBASE and FoxPro may have different rules for file names. If you aren't sure which format to select, stick with the default. Most database applications can work with dBASE IV files.

Follow these steps to name the new database:

1. In the New dialog box (shown in Figure 4.2), type the file name in the File name text box. If you want to use the default folder and file type, skip to step 4.

2. To save the database in another folder, select the folder from the list. You can use the Create in list to change to a drive or folder. Click the Up One Level button to move up one level in the folder structure.

3. To change the file format, display the Create type drop-down list and select the file type.

4. Click the Create button. Approach creates the database file.

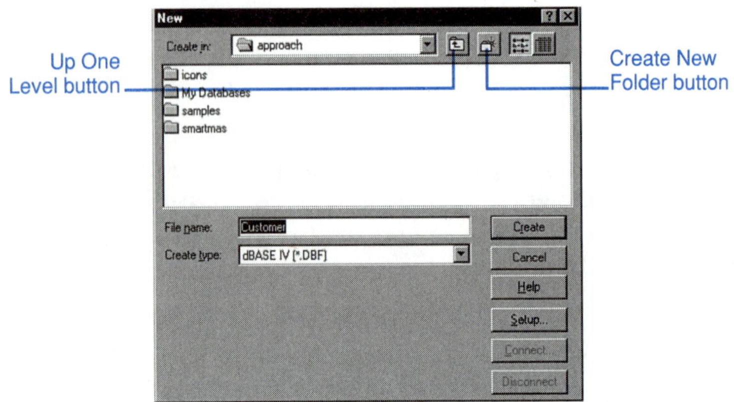

FIGURE 4.2 Type the name for the database.

Create a new folder You can create a new folder on the fly, right in the New dialog box. To do so, click the Create New Folder button, type the folder name, and click the OK button.

REVIEWING THE DATABASE

When you create a database using a SmartMaster, Approach first creates the necessary files and fields for the database. Also, Approach creates two default views: a form (named the same as the database and including all the fields) and a worksheet.

Before you begin using the new database, you should take some time to familiarize yourself with the structure. Figure 4.3 shows a Customer database. Notice the label or database title at the top; you can move or change the look of this element.

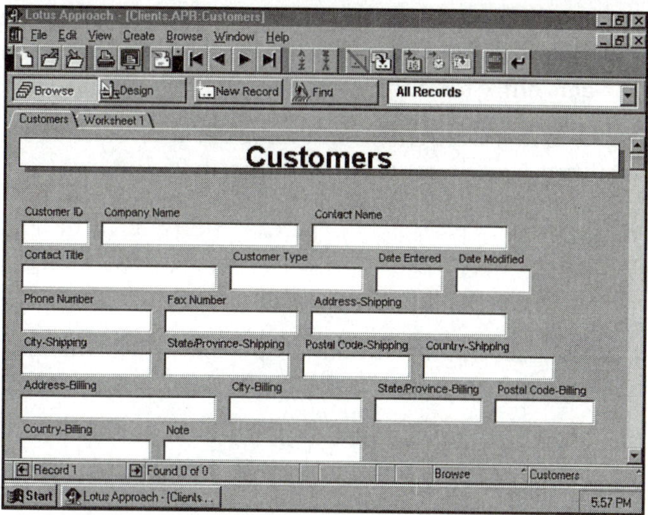

FIGURE 4.3 Take a look at the fields included in a SmartMaster database.

Notice all the fields. Each field has a field name and a field entry box. For some databases, you won't be able to see all the fields in one screen. You can scroll through the window by clicking the scroll arrows or dragging the scroll box to see all the fields. Also, take a look at the field order. On the default form, the fields are arranged in a certain order, which you will follow when you enter data. To try out the entry order, press Tab to move from field to field.

As you review the fields, you may find that the database isn't exactly what you need. Keep in mind the following:

- If the database includes fields you don't need, you can delete them.
- If you want to include some additional fields in the database, you can add them.

- Don't like the arrangement of the fields? Do you prefer a different order? If so, you can move the fields around on the data entry form so that they are in the order you like.
- Want to make the entry form more decorative? You can add logos and draw other objects on the form.

Modifying the form is covered in Lessons 15–18. Keep in mind that you should spend some time to get the database set up how you want before you start entering data.

The database does not include any data—only one blank record. You can add data, as covered in Lesson 6.

SAVING THE APPROACH FILE

The last step in setting up the database is to save the Approach (APR) file. Remember that this is the file that stores all the views and is separate from the database file. Even if you don't make any changes to any of the views, you still need to save and name this file. You can use the same name as the database file.

Follow these steps to save the Approach file:

1. Open the File menu and select the Save Approach File command. You see the Save Apr dialog box (see Figure 4.4).
2. In the File name text box, type a name for the Approach file.
3. If necessary, select another folder in which to place the file. You can double-click on any folders listed to open them. To move up one level in the folder structure, click the Up One Level button. To select another drive, use the Save in drop-down list.
4. Click the Save button. Approach saves the file.

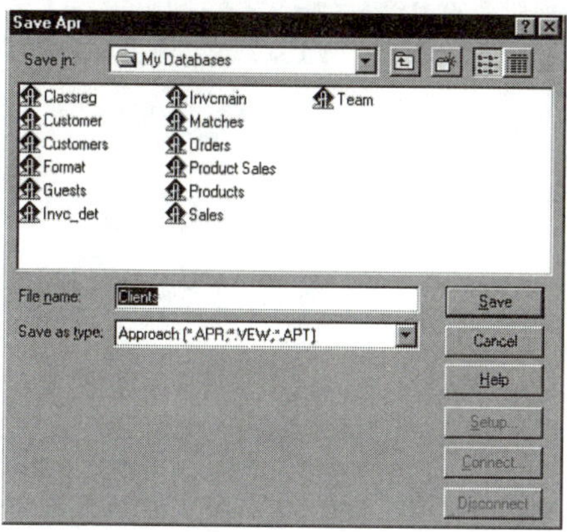

Figure 4.4 Type a name and select a folder for the Approach file.

Forget to save? If you forget to save and try to close the database or exit Approach, you will be prompted to save the file. You can select Yes to save the file, No to exit without saving, or Cancel to return to the database.

In this lesson, you learned how to create and save a new database using the SmartMaster. In the next lesson, you will learn a different method for creating a database.

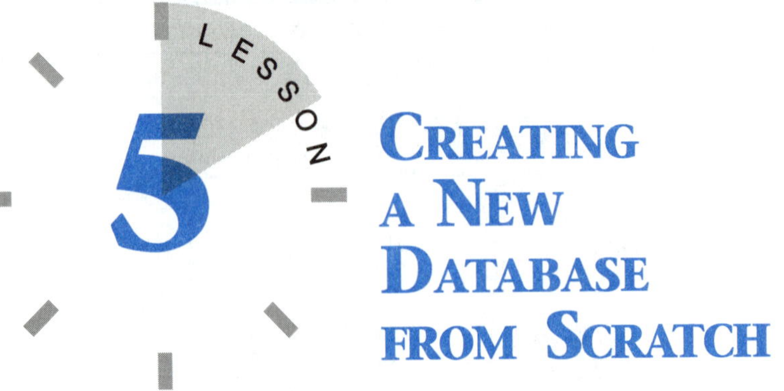

Creating a New Database from Scratch

In this lesson, you will learn how to create a blank database and then define the fields you want to include in this database.

Creating a Blank Database

If none of the SmartMasters suit your needs, you can create a blank database with no fields. You can then define the fields you want to include. This method for creating a new database makes sense if you would have to spend a lot of time modifying a SmartMaster. Also, some users like to use this method so that they can select the exact names and order for the fields.

Initially, the steps you follow to create a blank database are similar to using a SmartMaster. You select the blank database and then enter a name and select a folder for the database file. Follow these steps:

1. In the Welcome to Lotus Approach dialog box, click the Create a New File Using a SmartMaster tab (see Figure 5.1). The welcome dialog box is displayed when you start Approach or when you close all databases. You can also create a new database by opening the File menu and selecting the New Database command.
2. Select Blank Database (the default) and click the OK button. You see the New dialog box (see Figure 5.2).

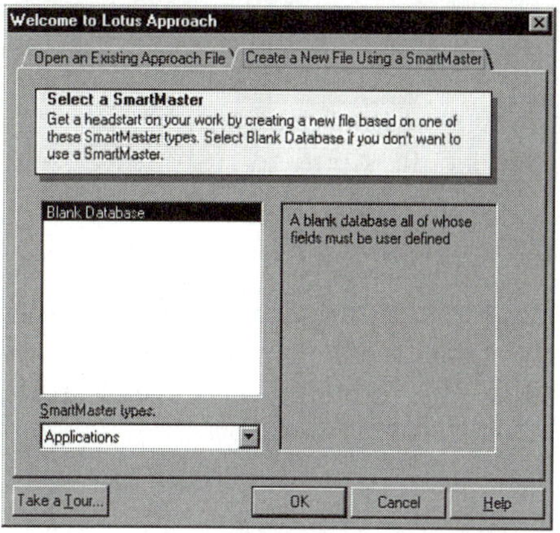

FIGURE 5.1 Select the SmartMaster you want to use from the list.

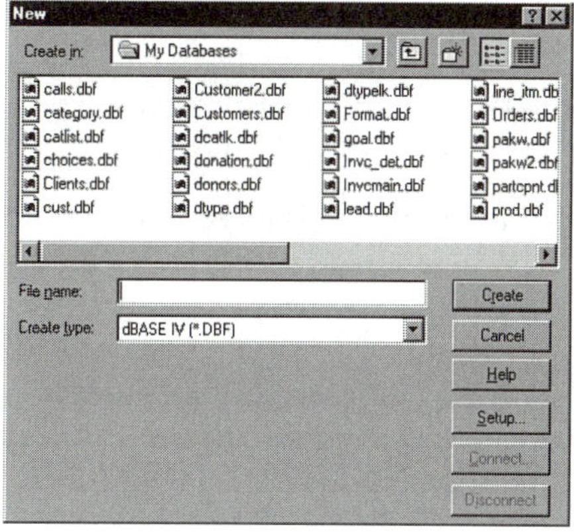

FIGURE 5.2 Type a name for the new database.

3. In the File name text box, type a name for the database file. You can type up to 255 characters, including spaces.
4. If necessary, select a different folder in which to save the file. If the folder is listed, you can double-click on it to open the folder. To move up one level in the folder

structure, click the Up One Level button. To change to a different drive, use the Create in drop-down list.

5. If necessary, select a file type from the Create type drop-down list. By default, Approach uses the dBASE IV file format. The file type affects the field options, such as field names, for the database.

6. Click the Create button. Approach displays the Creating New Database dialog box. In this dialog box, you build the fields you want to include, as covered in the next two sections.

UNDERSTANDING FIELD TYPES

As you know, a database is composed of several different fields (think of fields as compartments for data), each with a field name. When you create a field for a database, you first type a field name. You also select a field type; different fields can store different types of data. Finally, you can select a size (number of characters) for the field.

Before you start creating the fields in your database, take some time to review the different field types. The field type affects what you can enter in the field and how you can enter data in the field. For example, if you set up a date field, you can enter only numbers in the field, using a particular format. Table 5.1 describes each of the field types. Keep in mind that the file type you select affects some of the field options.

TABLE 5.1 FIELD TYPES

FIELD TYPE	DESCRIPTION
Text	A text field is the most common type of field and is the default field type. You can type any type of character (letters, numbers, symbols) in a text field, and you can select a size up to 254 characters.

continues

TABLE 5.1 CONTINUED

FIELD TYPE	DESCRIPTION
Numeric	You can store only numbers in a numeric field. Use this type of field for quantities, prices, and other numeric information. You can use this type of field in calculations. Also, you can specify the number of digits to the right and left of the decimal point for the field size.
Date	You can set up a date field to store one date. This type of field has a fixed field size.
Time	You can set up a time field to store a single time.
Memo	If you need to enter more than 254 characters in a field, you can create a memo field. The contents of this field is stored as a separate file.
PicturePlus	If you need to insert a picture or other graphic object (for example, a picture of a product or employee), use this field type. You can insert any type of object that supports OLE (Object Linking and Embedding).
Boolean	Use this type of field to store a yes (1) or no (0) response. For example, you might have a field in a guest list that says whether or not the guest is attending the event.
Calculated	In some cases, you will want to have a field that is actually the result of some calculation. For example, in an invoice database, you might have a total field that multiplies the number of units by the price. Creating calculated fields is covered in Lesson 14.

FIELD TYPE	DESCRIPTION
Variable	The contents of this field are stored only temporarily in memory, not on disk. The value in the variable field is the same for all records. Variable fields are often used in macros, which aren't covered in this book.

ADDING THE FIELDS

When you create and name a blank database, you see the Creating New Database dialog box (see Figure 5.3). This dialog box includes a grid of one row and four columns, like a worksheet. Here is where you enter the field name, data type, size, and formula/options for the fields.

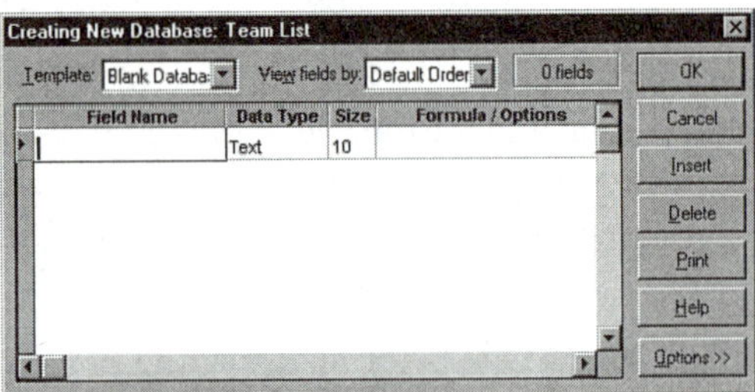

FIGURE 5.3 Set up the fields you want by typing a name, selecting a data type, and entering a field size.

This section covers how to enter the name, type, and size. See Lesson 14 for information on creating formulas and using some of the data entry and validation options.

Follow these steps to add a field:

1. In the Field Name column, type the name for the field. Depending on the file type, the length of the field name and the characters you can include will vary. For example, in dBASE IV files you can have field names

up to 32 characters; this can include any characters, including letters, numbers, spaces, commas, and periods.

2. Press Tab to move to the Data Type column. Notice this column displays an arrow, indicating a drop-down list (see Figure 5.4).

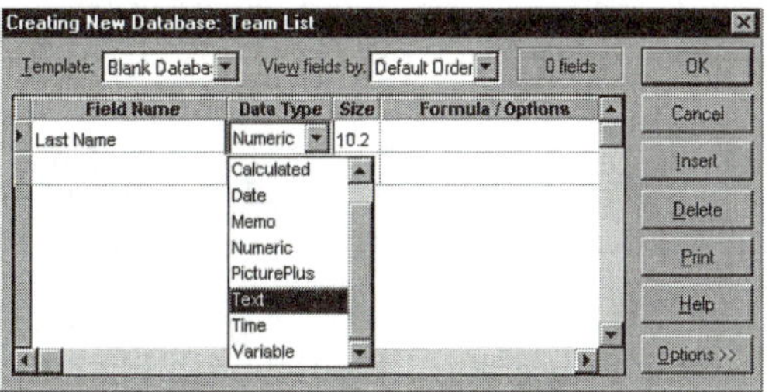

FIGURE 5.4 Select the data type from a drop-down list.

3. Display the drop-down list and select the data type you want. Or type the data type.

4. Press Tab to move to the Size column. Approach displays a default field size (depending on the data type). For most data types, the field size will be fixed. You can enter a size for text and numeric fields.

5. If necessary, type the field size.

6. Press Tab to move to the next row. Approach adds the field and moves to the next row.

7. Follow steps 1–6 to add all the fields you want to include.

8. When you are finished adding fields, click the OK button.

Tips for Creating Fields

When you are adding the fields for your database, keep in mind the following tips:

- For field names, use a name that is descriptive of the contents of the field. Try to keep the names short. Long field names will take up a lot of room on the entry form.
- Be sure to select an appropriate data type. Doing so will make sure that you (and other users) will make a correct entry. For example, if a field should contain a date, set it up as a date field so that only dates are accepted.
- Use numeric fields only for numbers that will be used in calculations or for sorting in numeric order. For example, because you won't sort or calculate phone numbers, you should set up a phone number as a text field rather than a numeric field.
- You can set up field options that will check the data that is entered or will automatically make an entry. These features are covered in Lesson 15.
- If you add a field by mistake, you can delete it. To do so, select the field (click anywhere in the field row) and click the Delete button.
- In a database, the fields will appear in the order you create them. Therefore, be sure to enter the fields in the order you want. If you need to insert a field within the existing fields, select the row you want. The new field will be inserted above the row. Then click the Insert button.
- You can change the order in which the fields are displayed in the dialog box. To do so, display the View fields by drop-down list and select an order. You may want to do this to group similar fields together when you are working on the field list. Keep in mind that changing this order doesn't affect the order of the fields in the database (only the dialog box).

- If you want a record of the fields, you can print the list. To do so, click the Print button.

Saving the Approach File

When you create a new database, Approach creates two default views (a form and a worksheet). Even if you don't make changes to these views, you still must save the view (APR) file before you exit. To do so, follow these steps:

1. Open the File menu and select the Save Approach File command. You see the Save Apr dialog box.
2. In the File name text box, type a name for the Approach file.
3. If necessary, select another folder in which to place the file. You can double-click on any folders listed to open them. To move up one level in the folder structure, click the Up One Level button. To select another drive, use the Save in drop-down list.
4. Click the Save button. Approach saves the file.

Forget to save? If you forget to save and try to close the database or exit Approach, you will be prompted to save the file. You can select Yes to save the file, No to exit without saving, or Cancel to return to the database.

In this lesson, you learned how to create a blank database and set up the fields you want to include. In the next lesson, you will learn how to add records to an existing database.

Adding Records

In this lesson, you will learn how to enter data into your fields and create records.

What Is a Form?

When you create a new database, you see the default data entry form, which contains all the fields in the database in the order you created them. In most cases, this is the form you will use to enter data.

To enter data, you have to be in Browse mode, which is the default mode after you create a new database. If you have made some design changes to the form (switching to Design mode), you can switch back to Browse by clicking the Browse button in the action bar or by opening the View menu and selecting the Browse & Data Entry command.

Form A *form* is a view of a database that shows one record at a time. You can use this view to enter and edit records.

Just browsing The keyboard shortcut for changing to Browse mode is Ctrl+B.

The database contains one blank record. You can use this record to start entering data. After you complete one record, you can add another and so on until you get all the data you want entered.

Note that in addition to the default form, Approach creates a worksheet. You can use this view to enter data into a column and row structure. Using a worksheet is covered in Lesson 24. If you don't want to see all the fields, you can create a new form or customize the default form. You can then use one of these forms to enter data. Customizing forms is the topic of Lessons 12–18.

ENTERING DATA IN FIELDS

Entering data into a record is simple: just type the entry for one field, then press Tab or Enter to move to the next field. Approach moves through the fields in the order you created them.

When you type the entry, you have to be sure to do it in an acceptable format. The following steps give you an overview of the process. The remaining sections discuss specific formats for different data types in more detail.

To enter data into a blank record, follow these steps:

1. Click in the field. The insertion point appears in the selected field (see Figure 6.1).
2. Enter the data using the appropriate format. The format you follow depends on the field's data type.

Hear a beep? If you type an unacceptable entry, Approach beeps and displays an error message. Review the message and then type the entry in the proper format.

Move backwards Press Shift+Tab to move backwards through the fields.

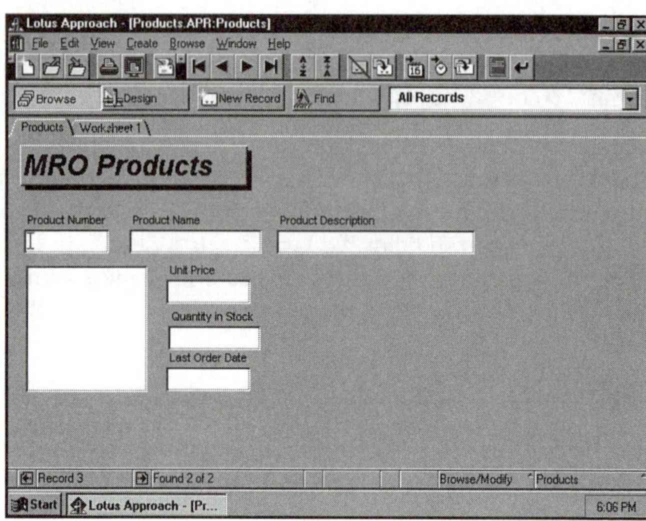

FIGURE 6.1 The first field is selected.

3. Press Tab to move to the next field. Or click in the next field.
4. Continue typing entries and pressing Tab until you complete all the fields in the record.

ENTERING DATA IN A TEXT OR MEMO FIELD

In a text or memo field, you can type any characters that you want, up to the limit you set when you defined the field. For example, if you have a text field that is 10 characters, you can type only 10 characters. If you type 11, Approach displays an error message. Click the OK button and stick to the limits.

ENTERING NUMBERS IN A NUMERIC FIELD

In a numeric field, you can enter only numbers and a decimal point, up to the field size. For example, if you have a field size that limits the entry to 5 characters to the left of the decimal place and 2 to the right (indicated as 5.2), you can type only entries equal to or smaller than 99999.99.

When you enter a value in a numeric field, you can type the period, but don't type a comma, percent sign, or dollar sign. Instead, change the format of the field so that these elements are displayed automatically. Changing the format of a field is covered in Lesson 15.

ENTERING A BOOLEAN FIELD

To complete a Boolean field, you can type Yes, Y, yes, y, or 1 for true. No matter which entry you choose, Approach will display the value as Yes. For a false entry, you can type No, N, no, n, or 0. Approach displays the value as No.

ENTERING DATES AND TIMES

To enter a date, type it in the format *mm/dd/yy*. You don't have to type the slashes which separate the date elements.

Current date and time You can enter the current date and time by clicking the Date and Time icons, respectively. You can also press the space bar in a date or time field to enter the current date or time.

To enter a time, type up to 12 characters in the format *hh:mm:ss*. You don't have to type the seconds or the colons.

You can control how dates and times are displayed by changing the date or time format, as covered in Lesson 16.

ENTERING A PICTURE

If you have included a PicturePlus field in your database, you can use one of several methods to add the picture to the record. You can copy and paste the picture or import the picture.

To copy and paste a picture, follow these steps:

1. Open the application you used to create the picture and then select it.
2. Open the Edit menu and select the Copy command.
3. Switch back to Approach and select the PicturePlus field.
4. Open the Edit menu and select the Paste command. The object is pasted into the record.

Use Paste Special If you want more control over how the object is pasted, select the Paste Special command. Using this command, you can specify how the object is pasted and whether it is linked to the original. Make your selections and click OK.

If you don't want to have to open the picture application, you can simply import the picture by following these steps:

1. Select the PicturePlus field.
2. Open the Edit menu, select the Picture command, then select the Import command. You see the Import Picture dialog box.
3. Change to the drive and folder that contain the picture. Then select the picture file type and the picture you want (see Figure 6.2).

Change the file types If you want to change the types of files that are listed, display the Files type drop-down list and select the file type you want.

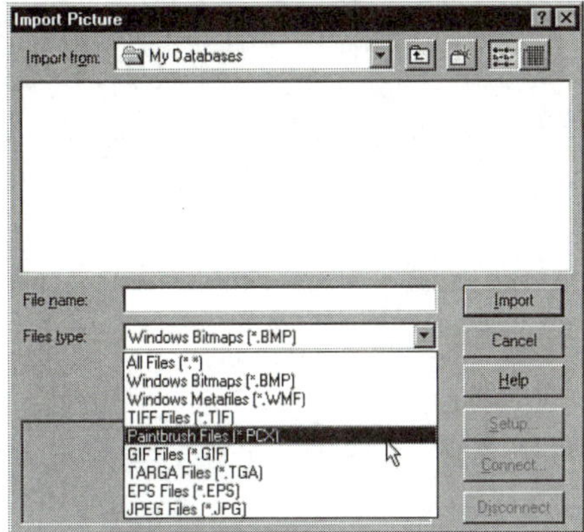

FIGURE 6.2 Use the Import Picture dialog box to import a picture to a PicturePlus field.

4. Click the Import button. Approach imports the picture into the current PicturePlus field (see Figure 6.3).

SAVING AND ADDING THE RECORD

When you get to the last field in the last record and press Tab, Approach does a couple of things. First, Approach displays a new blank record. You can continue completing the fields and adding records. You can also add a new record by clicking the New Record button in the action bar, by clicking the New Record icon in the icon bar, or by opening the Browse menu and selecting the New Record command.

Try a keyboard shortcut? If you prefer to use the keyboard over icons, you can press Ctrl+N to insert a new record.

Second, Approach saves the database and the record. You don't have to do anything special to save the database as you add records.

FIGURE 6.3 You can insert a picture using a PicturePlus field.

Where's the Browse menu? The name of the Browse menu may vary, depending on the current field. For example, if you are in a PicturePlus field, the menu name is PicturePlus. Approach calls this changing menu the context menu. This book refers to it as the Browse menu.

In this lesson, you learned how to add a record to your database. The next lesson explains how to make editing changes to your records.

Editing Data

In this lesson, you will learn some techniques for editing the data in records. You start by learning how to open a database. Then you'll learn how to make corrections and check spelling.

Opening a Database

When you create a new database, Approach displays a blank record on-screen. You can start entering records right away in that database. If you've closed the database for some reason, you can open it and then enter new records or edit existing records.

To open a database, follow these steps:

1. In the Welcome to Approach dialog box, take a look at the list of most recently opened databases. (If this dialog box isn't displayed, open the File menu and select the Open command.) If you see the one you want listed, click on it and skip the remaining steps.
2. If the database isn't listed, click the Browse For More Files button. Approach displays the Open dialog box (see Figure 7.1).
3. Change to the drive and folder that contain your database. To select a different drive, you can display the Drives drop-down list. To change to a different folder, double-click on the folder in the list. Use the Up One Level button to move up a level in the folder structure.

4. Select the database you want to open and then click the Open button. Approach opens the database and displays the first record.

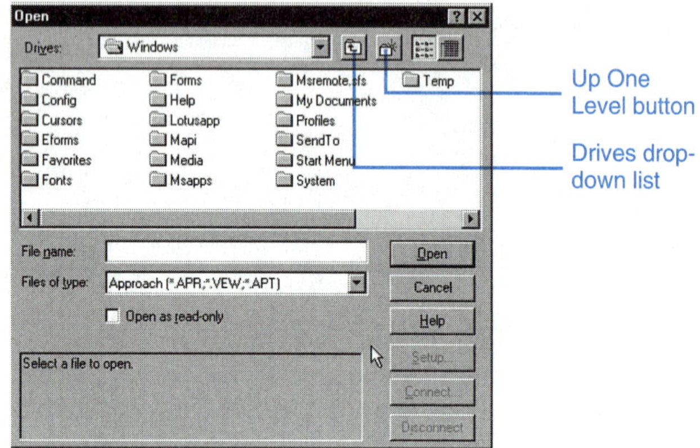

FIGURE 7.1 You can open a database using this dialog box.

MAKING CORRECTIONS

If you make a mistake while typing an entry, you have several options for correcting the mistake.

If you type something incorrectly, you can press Backspace to delete characters to the left of the insertion point and then retype the entry.

If you didn't notice the mistake until after you've entered it:

1. Click in the field where you want to make the change. You can place the insertion point at the exact point where you want to make the correction, or click anywhere in the field and then use the arrow keys to move the insertion point.
2. You can make corrections in two ways:
    - Press Delete to delete characters to the right of the insertion point.

- Press Backspace to delete characters to the left of the insertion point.

If you need to replace the entire entry, follow these steps:

1. Drag the insertion point across the text so that it is highlighted.

Quick select Press Tab to move to a field and select the entire contents.

2. Press Delete to delete it.

Erase and replace When you start typing within a selected field, the new entry automatically replaces the old one.

CHECKING SPELLING

When you use your data in reports or to create form letters, you will want to be sure that the data is spelled correctly. Nothing says sloppiness more than a typographical error.

In Browse mode, Approach checks the spelling of all records. You can also run the spell-checker in Design mode to check the spelling of your field labels and text objects in the form or report.

The spelling program works by comparing the entries in your database to those in its dictionary. Any words the speller can't find are flagged and displayed. That doesn't necessarily mean the word is misspelled; it just means the Approach speller can't find the word. You select how to handle the flagged word and then Approach moves on to the next word, until all the words are checked.

Follow these steps to check the spelling:

1. Click the Spell Check icon or open the Edit menu and select the Check Spelling command. You see the Spell Check dialog box (see Figure 7.2).

Keyboard shortcut Press Ctrl+F2 to start the speller.

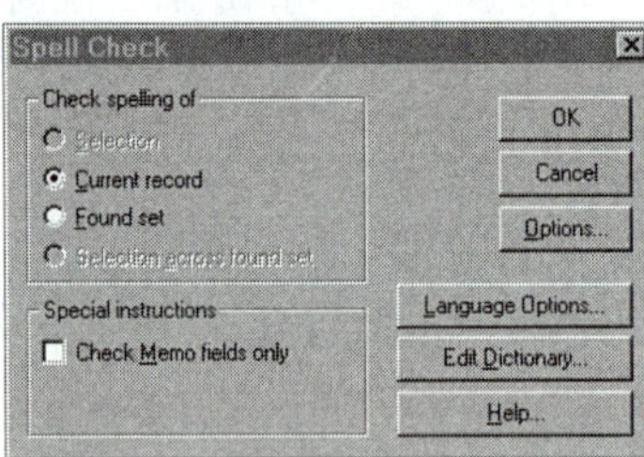

FIGURE 7.2 Select what you want to check.

2. In the dialog box, select what you want to check (just the current selection, the current record, the found set, or a selection across the found set).
3. Click OK. Approach starts the speller and flags any questionable spellings. The dialog box lists any alternative spellings for the questionable word.
4. Do one of the following for each word flagged:
    - If the word is spelled incorrectly and the correct spelling appears in the Alternatives list, click on the word you want to use as the replacement. Then click the Replace button to replace this occurrence. Click the Replace All button to replace all occurrences.

- If the word is spelled incorrectly, but the correct spelling isn't listed in the Alternatives list, edit the word in the Replace with text box so that it is spelled correctly. Then click the Replace or Replace All button.
- If the word is spelled correctly, click the Skip button to skip this occurrence. Click the Skip All button to skip all occurrences of this word.
- To add the word to the dictionary so that it is not flagged again, click the Add To Dictionary button.

5. After all the words are checked, you see an alert box. Click OK to close this dialog box.

In this lesson, you learned how to edit data in your database. The next lesson explains some shortcuts for entering data.

Data Entry Shortcuts

In this lesson, you will learn some shortcuts for entering data into a record.

Duplicating a Record

In some cases, you may enter similar records in your database. For example, suppose that you use a database to keep track of contacts, and you have several contacts from the same company (with the same company name, address information, and phone numbers). You could create each record and type the same information over and over. Or you can use a shortcut: you can duplicate the record and then edit the duplicate.

Follow these steps:

1. Display the record you want to duplicate.
2. Click the Duplicate Current Record icon in the icon bar or open the Browse menu and select the Duplicate Record command. Approach creates a new record using the same values from the original record. The insertion point is in the first field.
3. Make any corrections to the duplicate.

Duplicating a Value from a Previous Record

In addition to duplicating all the values in a record, you can simply duplicate a value from a field. Approach will use the value from the same field of the preceding record (the one you just entered).

To duplicate a value, follow these steps:

1. Create the new record by clicking the New Record button or by pressing Ctrl+N.
2. Enter the values you want. When you get to the field where you want to duplicate the value, open the Browse menu, select the Insert command, and select the Previous Value command. Or press Ctrl+Shift+P.

INSERTING THE DATE AND TIME

If your database includes date and time fields, you may often need to insert the current date and time. Approach provides shortcuts for entering these values. To enter the current date, open the Browse menu, select Insert, and then select Today's Date. Or press Ctrl+Shift+D. To insert the current time, open the Browse menu, select Insert, and then select Current Time. Or press Ctrl+Shift+T.

Date and time wrong? If the date and time entered are wrong, you need to adjust your system date and time. To do so, right-click on the clock in the taskbar and select Adjust Date/Time. In the dialog box that appears, make any changes to the time and/or date and then click OK.

USING THE ICON BAR FOR DATA ENTRY SHORTCUTS

Approach provides several methods to accomplish the same task. For example, you can use a menu command, a keyboard shortcut, or an icon bar to duplicate a value. Take a look at the following icons, which are useful for duplicating and quickly entering values:

ICON	DESCRIPTION
	Duplicates the preceding record
	Inserts today's date
	Inserts today's time
	Duplicates the value from the field in the preceding record in the field in the current record

FILLING A FIELD

In some cases, you may want to use the same value for a field throughout your database. For example, if all your clients are in Indiana, you could enter **IN** as the entry for the State field. You can enter a field automatically by filling a field (covered here) or by defining the default entry (covered in Lesson 15).

When you fill a field, keep in mind that Approach will use this value for all fields in all records. If the record contains a value, Approach will overwrite that value with the one you selected as the fill.

Follow these steps to fill a field:

1. Open the Browse menu and select the Fill Field command. You see the Fill Field dialog box (see Figure 8.1).
2. In the Field list, select the field you want to fill.
3. In the To the following text box, type the entry you want to use.
4. Click OK. Approach fills the selected field in all records with your entry.

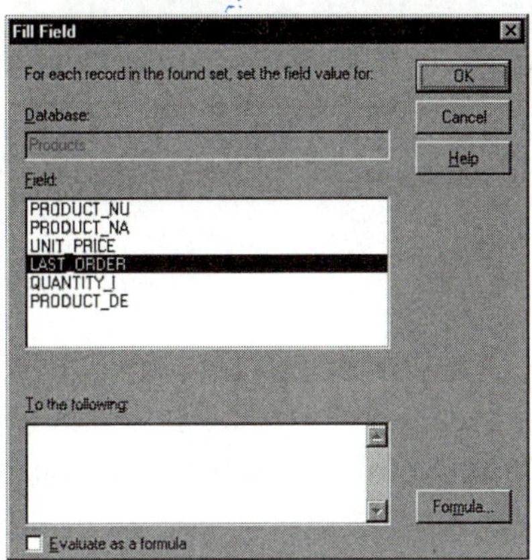

FIGURE 8.1 Select the field to fill and enter the value to use.

In this lesson, you learned some shortcuts for entering data. The next lesson shows how to move among records, delete records, and hide records.

LESSON

9 Working with Records

In this lesson, you will learn some techniques for working with the records in your database. You learn how to move among the records, delete records, and hide records.

Moving Among Records

In the default form, you see and work with only one record at a time—the current record that is displayed. The status bar displays the current record number, and records appear in the order you entered them.

When you want to review the information or make a change to another record, you need a way to display that record. Approach provides many different ways for scrolling through the records in your database. You can move through the records one at a time, you can move to the first or last record, and you can move to a particular record.

Scrolling Through Records

You can move around using the icon bar or the keyboard:

To move to	Click this	Or press
First record	|◀	Ctrl+Home
Previous record	◀	Page Up
Next record	▶	Page Down
Last record	▶|	Ctrl+End

You can also use the arrows in the status bar to move to the next or previous record.

GOING TO A SPECIFIC RECORD

If you have a lot of records, scrolling through them one at a time can take a lot of time. Instead, you can jump to a particular record number by following these steps:

1. Click the record number in the status bar. You see the Go to Record dialog box (see Figure 9.1).

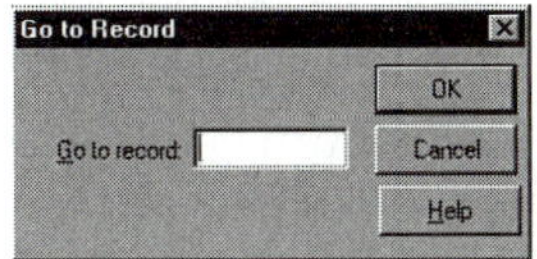

FIGURE 9.1 Use this dialog box to jump to a particular record.

2. Type the record number that you want to display.
3. Click OK or press Return. Approach displays that record.

Find a record quickly If you have many records and are searching for a particular one, use Find to search for the record, as described in the next lesson. Using Find will help you locate the record faster than scrolling through all of the records until you find the one you want.

DELETING A RECORD

One of the tasks you will need to do periodically is go through your database and delete records that you don't need. You may have entered a record by mistake, or perhaps you don't need the information in the record. Getting rid of unnecessary records keeps the database working more efficiently.

Follow these steps to delete a record:

1. Display the record you want to delete.
2. Click the Delete Record icon or open the Browse menu and select the Delete Record command. You are prompted to confirm the deletion.
3. Click Yes.

Shortcut You can press Ctrl+Delete to delete a record.

HIDING A RECORD

In some cases, you may want to hide a particular record. A hidden record isn't displayed when you browse through the records and it isn't printed when you print the database. Follow these steps:

1. Display the record you want to hide.
2. Open the Browse menu and select the Hide Record command or press Ctrl+H.

Another way to hide certain records is to use Find to display only a certain set of records. For example, you could choose to display all clients in Indiana; all other records would not be included in the resulting find set. For information on finding records, see the next lesson.

To redisplay all the records, open the Browse menu, select the Find command, and then select the Find All command. Or press Ctrl+A.

In this lesson you learned how to move among records, delete records, and hide records. The next lesson shows how to find records.

LESSON 10

Finding Records

In this lesson, you will learn how to search for a particular record or group of records in your database.

Creating a Find Request

If you have just a few records in your database, you can easily scroll through the records to find the one you want. If you have a lot of records, on the other hand, scrolling can take too much time. Instead, you can use a different method to find the record: you can create a find request.

When you create a find request, Approach creates a find set, which may be a single record or a group of records that match the conditions you enter. You can then scroll through this subset of records until you find the one you want.

Another reason you may want to create a find request is to group records together. For example, if you are a sales rep about to go on a sales trip, you may want to group all of your clients in a particular city. You can then print or work with this smaller list.

You have many options for searching. You can search on a single field or more than one field. And you can search for a particular entry or a range of entries, as covered in this lesson.

Searching on a Single Field

If you are just looking for a certain record, the fastest way is to create a simple find request and search for a particular value. Follow these steps:

1. Open the Browse menu, select the Find command, and then select Find. Or click the Find button in the action bar. Approach displays a blank record, with buttons for creating the find request in the action bar and icon bar (see Figure 10.1).

Other shortcuts You can also press Ctrl+F or click the Browse button in the status bar and select Find.

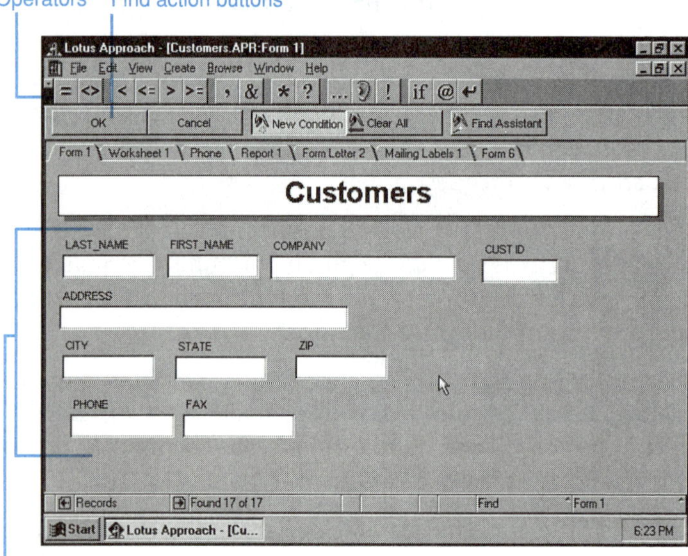

FIGURE 10.1 Create a find request by entering a value in any one of the database fields.

2. Click in the field that you want to search on and then enter the value you want to find.

3. Click OK in the action bar. Approach searches the database and displays matching records. Notice that the status

bar displays the number of found records. Also, if you scroll through these records, only records that match the find request are displayed.

REDISPLAYING ALL RECORDS

Keep in mind that Approach will display only the matching records until you tell the program to redisplay all records. If the search doesn't turn out as you planned, you can start over again by redisplaying all records. After you finish working with the found records, you will also want to return to a complete record set.

To do so, open the Browse menu, select Find, and select Find All. Or press Ctrl+A.

Sorts and finds not working If you find that a search or a sort doesn't work as you expected, make sure that you started with a complete set of records (not with a find set). Try redisplaying all records and then performing the find or sort again.

MATCHING MORE THAN ONE CONDITION

In some cases, you may want to match more than one condition. For example, you may want to list all clients in Charleston assigned to the sales rep Sigmon. If both conditions must be met, you can create an And search. For example, Approach would display only records that have both Charleston as the city and Sigmon as the sales rep.

If only one of two conditions must be met, you create an Or search. In this type of search, you can match either of the conditions or both. For example, Approach would include in the find set any record with Charleston as the city or Sigmon as the sales rep.

You can create an And or Or search using the blank find form or by using the Find Assistant. Because the Find Assistant leads you through the steps, this method is easier and is covered here. Follow these steps:

1. Open the Browse menu and select the Find command. From the submenu, select Find Assistant. Or from a find request, click the Find Assistant button. Approach displays the Find/Sort Assistant dialog box (see Figure 10.2). As the first step, select the type of find.

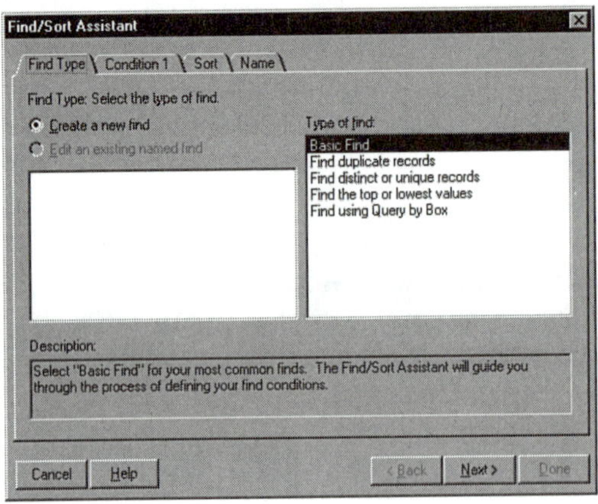

FIGURE 10.2 Select the type of find.

2. Keep the default (Basic Find) as the Find Type and then click on the Next button. Approach displays the Condition 1 tab (see Figure 10.3). Here you can enter the first condition.
3. Select the field to search on in the field list.
4. Select the operator from the Operator list.
5. Enter the value to match in the Values list box. Notice that Approach puts the condition into words and displays this text description in the dialog box. Use this description to check to make sure the search is what you intended.

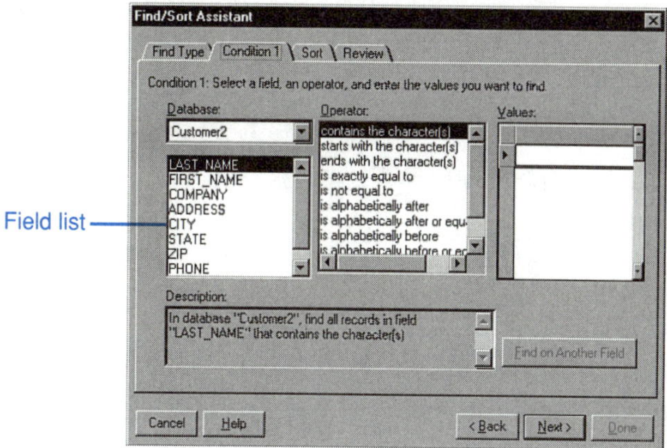

FIGURE 10.3 Select the field and operator and enter the value to match.

6. To create the next condition, click the Find on Another Field button. Approach displays the Condition 2 tab (see Figure 10.4).
7. Select the type of search: Find More (Or) or Find Fewer (And).
8. Follow steps 3–5 to create the next condition.
9. When you are finished creating conditions, click on the Next button. Approach prompts you to select a sort order. (This step is optional.)

Make a mistake? If you make a mistake, you can back up through the Find Assistant steps by clicking on the Back button. To delete a condition that you created by mistake, display the condition and then click the Delete Condition button.

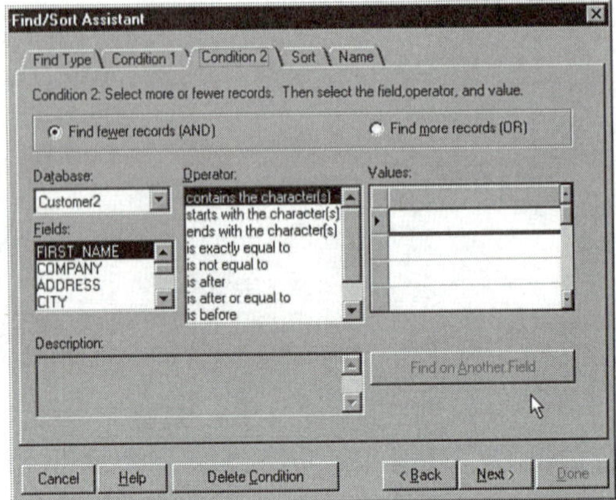

FIGURE 10.4 Enter the second condition.

10. Select a sort field if you want. Then click the Next button. (Sorting is covered in the next lesson.) Approach displays the Review tab (see Figure 10.5).
11. Review the search conditions. Then click the Done button to execute the search.

Save a search If you use the same find request often, you can save it. To do so, check the Named Find/Sort check box on the Review tab. Then enter a name and click the Done button. If you save a find request, you can select it from the drop-down list in the action bar on the far right edge.

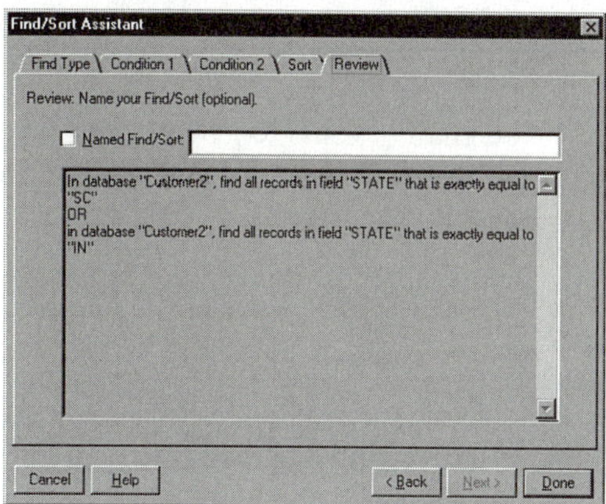

FIGURE 10.5 Use this tab to review the conditions and name the find request.

SEARCHING FOR A RANGE OF VALUES

For some searches, you may want to display a range of values—for instance, all sales orders over $1,200 or all clients that start with T or all bills past a certain date. You can search for a range using comparison operators.

You can select these operators from the Operator list if you use the Find Assistant. Or you can type the operator and value to match in the find form. Depending on the type of field, the operators you can use will vary. Table 8.1 describes each of the operators.

TABLE 8.1 OPERATORS

OPERATOR	EXPLANATION
<	Less than. For example, in an order database, type **<50** to find all orders less than 50.
>	Greater than. For example, in an order database, type **>500** to find all orders over 500.

continues

TABLE 8.1 CONTINUED

OPERATOR	EXPLANATION
<=	Less than or equal to. For example, in an order database, type **<=50** to find all orders less than or equal to 50.
>=	Greater than or equal to. For example in an order database, type **>=500** to list all orders greater than or equal to 500.
=	Equal to. For example, in a price database, type **=35.99** to find all products that are priced at 35.99.
<>	Not equal to. For example, in a team database, type **<>3** in the rating field to find all team players not rated 3.
...	Range of values. For example, type **R...T** in a product name field to find all products that start with R, S, or T.
*	Wildcard that can match one or more characters. For example, T* in a text field finds all entries that start with T.
?	Wildcard that matches a single character. For example, PROD1? would find all products that have the product number PROD1 and some other number or character (PROD11, PROD12, and so on).
!	Makes the search case-sensitive. For example, !Dunlop matches Dunlop, but not dunlop or DUNLOP.

Find blank fields Type **=** in a field and perform the search to find all records that have a blank entry for that field. You can use this type of search to complete any partial records.

SEARCHING FOR DUPLICATE RECORDS

One of the things you should do to keep your database operating smoothly is to check for duplicate records and get rid of any duplicates. You can create a special type of find request for duplicates by following these steps:

1. Open the Browse menu and select the Find command. From the submenu, select Find Assistant. Or from a find request, click the Find Assistant button. Approach displays the Find/Sort Assistant dialog box.
2. Select Find duplicate records from the Type of find list. Then click the Next button. Approach prompts you to select the field you want to check. You can check more than one field for duplicate entries.
3. Select the field to check and click the Add button. Do this for each field you want to check for duplicate values. When you have selected all the fields, click the Next button.
4. Approach prompts you to select a sort order (optional). Select a sort field if you want and click the Next button. (Sorting is covered in the next lesson.)
5. Approach displays the Review tab. Review the search conditions. Then click the Done button to execute the search. Approach creates a find set with any duplicate records. If there are no duplicate records, Approach displays an error message.

Delete a found set If you want to delete a set of found records, you can do so by opening the Browse menu and selecting the Delete Found Set command.

In this lesson you learned how to search for a single record or group of records using one of several types of find requests. In the next lesson you learn how to sort the records in your database.

Sorting Records

In this lesson, you will learn how to sort your records using different sort orders.

Sorting Records in Ascending or Descending Order

If you scroll through the records in a database, you'll notice that they appear in the order you entered them. That doesn't mean that you have to arrange records before you enter them. With Approach, you can enter your records in any order and then rearrange them using a sort.

The fastest way to sort is to select a single field and sort on it. For example, you can arrange a customer database by last name by sorting on the last name field. Follow these steps:

1. Click in the field you want to sort on.
2. Click the Ascending Sort or Descending Sort icon. Or open the Browse menu and select Find and then Ascending or Descending.

Depending on the type of field you selected and the sort order, Approach reorders the records.

Command dim? If the Ascending and Descending commands are dim, it means you have not selected a field to search on. Be sure to click within the field to select the field to sort.

ORDER	TYPE OF FIELD	ORDER
Ascending		
	Text	A to Z
	Numeric	Lowest to highest
	Date and Time	Earliest to latest
Descending		
	Text	Z to A
	Numeric	Highest to lowest
	Date and Time	Latest to earliest

SORTING ON MORE THAN ONE FIELD

In some cases you may want to sort on more than one field. For example, in a customer database, you may want to sort on last name and then first name. As another option, you may want to sort on city to group all customers in the same city. Within that grouping, you may want to sort on last name to put the customers in alphabetical order.

To sort on more than one field, follow these steps:

1. Open the Browse menu, select the Sort command, and select the Define command. Approach displays the Sort dialog box (see Figure 11.1).

Keyboard shortcut Press Ctrl+T to display the Sort dialog box.

2. In the Fields list, click on the first field you want to sort on. Then click the Add button.

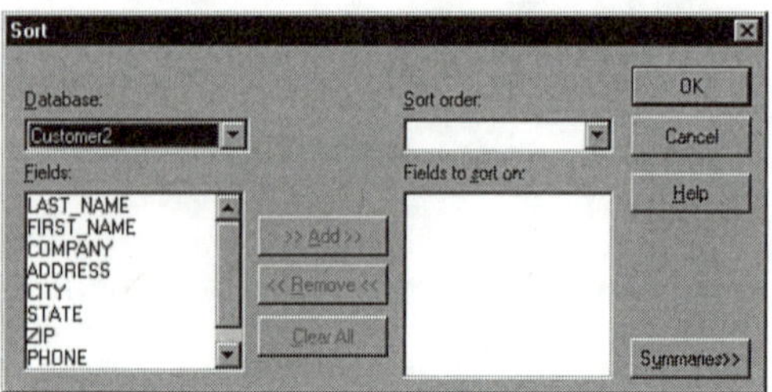

FIGURE 11.1 Select the fields to sort on.

3. Continue selecting a field and clicking the Add button until you add all the fields on which you want to sort.
4. Display the Sort order drop-down list and select a sort order: Ascending or Descending.
5. Click OK. Approach sorts the records on the fields in the order you selected.

Remove a field To remove a field added to the sort list by accident, click on the field in the Fields to sort on list and then click the Remove button. To clear all fields from this list, click the Clear All button.

SETTING A DEFAULT ORDER

If you want, you can set a default order that will be used for the database. This order will be used each time you open the database, but keep in mind that you can still sort to change the default order.

Follow these steps to set a default order:

1. Open the File menu, select User Setup, and then select Approach Preferences. You see the Approach Preferences dialog box.
2. Select the Order tab (see Figure 11.2).

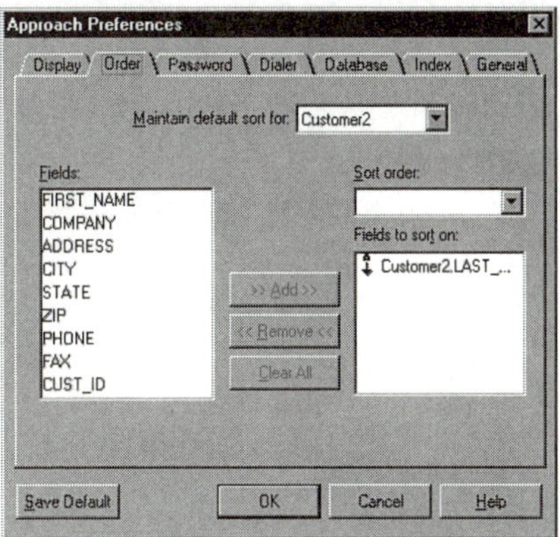

Figure 11.2 Use the Order tab to set a default order for your database.

3. In the Fields list, select the first field to sort on and then click the Add button. Do this for each field you want to sort on.

4. Click OK. Approach sorts the database using the default sort order you selected.

In this lesson you learned how to sort your records. The next lesson covers how to use design view to customize or create a new form or report.

LESSON 12

Working in Design View

In this lesson, you will learn some techniques for working in design view. This view is used to create and customize forms and reports.

When You Use Design View

Approach includes a default form and worksheet when you create a new database. When you first get started, these may be the only types of views you need. For instance, the default form may be perfect for data entry.

As you become more proficient, you may find that you want to do more with Approach or that you want to do things differently. For example, you may wish the form was set up differently. Or you may want to create a report of your top clients. Or you may want to add or delete fields on the database. In all of these cases, you start by changing to Design view.

The rest of this book covers how to make specific changes—how to create a report, how to add fields, and so on. This lesson introduces you to this view and explains some of the skills you can use to work in this view. These skills pertain to all the different types of changes you may make (reports, forms, and so on).

Changing to Design View

When you are working with records, you have to be in Browse mode. There are certain tasks—for instance, adding new records—that can only be done in Browse. On the other hand, when you want to make a change to the structure of a view, you need to switch to Design view. There are certain tasks—such as adding a new database field—that can only be done in Design view. The status bar displays the current mode.

You can use any of the following methods for switching to Design view:

- Click the Design button in the action bar.
- Click the Browse status bar button and select Design.
- Open the View menu and select Design.
- Press Ctrl+D.

In design view, Approach displays the current form on a dotted grid (see Figure 12.1). The status bar displays the horizontal and vertical positions of the mouse pointer. You can use this information as you draw and move items on the form. The rest of this lesson describes some of the tools and views you can work with in Design.

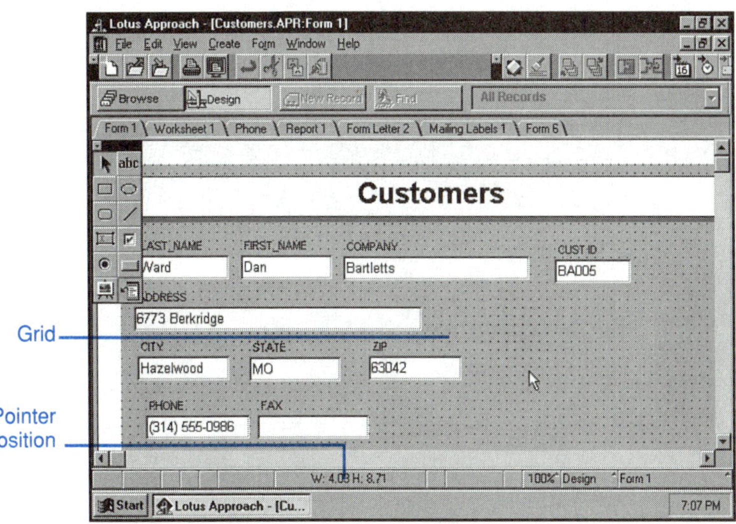

FIGURE 12.1 A form in Design view.

ZOOMING THE DISPLAY

When you are working in Design view, you may want to enlarge or make smaller the display for several reasons. For example, in a large report, you may be able to see only part of the report on-screen. To get an overall view of the entire page, you can change the view by zooming out. If you are drawing on a form, on the other hand, you may want a close-up view. In this case, you can zoom in.

Approach provides several different zoom options. Zoom in or out by following these steps:

1. Open the View menu.
2. Do one of the following:
   - To zoom in, select the Zoom In command.
   - To zoom out, select the Zoom Out command.
   - To zoom to a certain percentage, select the Zoom To command. Then select the zoom percentage: 25%, 50%, 75%, 85%, 100%, or 200%.

Figure 12.2 shows a form zoomed to 200%.

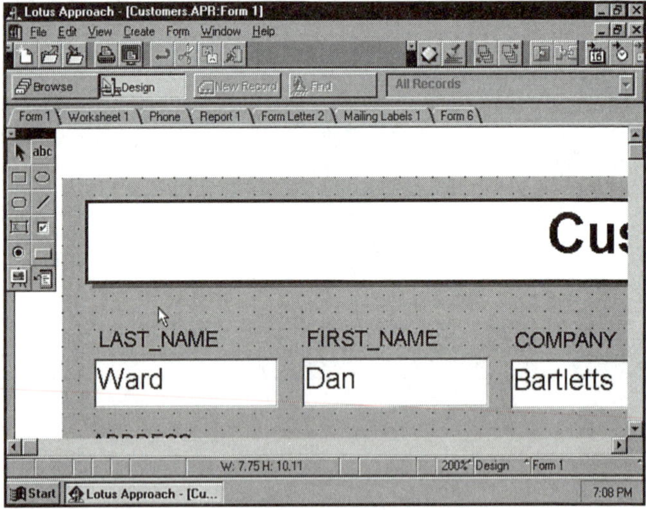

FIGURE 12.2 Zoom in to see a close-up.

Aligning Objects

When you are placing objects on the form, you usually want to keep them aligned. Approach provides several different view tools for aligning objects. When a command is on, you see a checkmark next to it. You can select the command again to turn the item off.

- By default, the form or report is displayed on a dotted grid. If you want to turn off the grid, open the View menu and uncheck the Show Grid command.
- If you have trouble placing objects exactly where you want them on the grid, you can have Approach snap them to the nearest grid point. Doing so helps keep the items in an exact alignment. To turn on this option, open the View menu and select the Snap to Grid command.
- As another alignment tool, you can display rulers on-screen and then use the rulers to place items at a certain measurement on the form or report. To use this option, open the View menu and select the Show Rulers command.

Figure 12.3 shows Design view with the rulers turned on.

Checking Fields

Two other options on the View menu help you check the fields included in the form. You can use the Show Data command in the View menu to show the actual contents of the fields. When this item is not selected, you see the field names.

To check the tab order (the order that you use to enter data), open the View menu and select the Show Tab Order command. Approach displays numbers in each of the fields, which indicate the tab order.

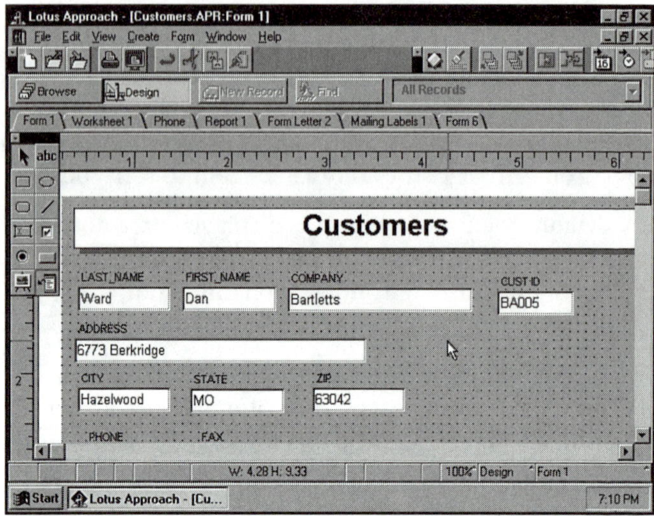

FIGURE 12.3 Use the rulers to align items on the form.

USING THE TOOLS PALETTE

In many cases, you will be adding items to the view. For example, you may want to draw an object on the form or add a field. To help you add new items, you can display and use the Tools palette. To display this palette, open the View menu and select Show Tools Palette. Other lessons in this book provide specific instructions on using each of these buttons on the palette. As a reference, you can review the following table, which identifies each tool.

TOOL	USE TO
	Select objects
	Draw text blocks
	Draw squares and rectangles
	Draw circles and ellipses

TOOL	USE TO
	Draw rounded rectangles
	Draw lines
	Add fields
	Add check boxes
	Add option buttons
	Add macro buttons
	Add a PicturePlus field
	Display the Add Field dialog box

SELECTING AN OBJECT

When you work in Design view, you first select the item you want to modify. For example, if you want to move a field, you first select the field. If you want to make a label bold, you select the label. The remaining chapters describe how to make changes once the object is selected; here you learn how to simply select the object.

To select an object in Design view, click on it. Approach displays selection handles around the edges of the object (see Figure 12.4).

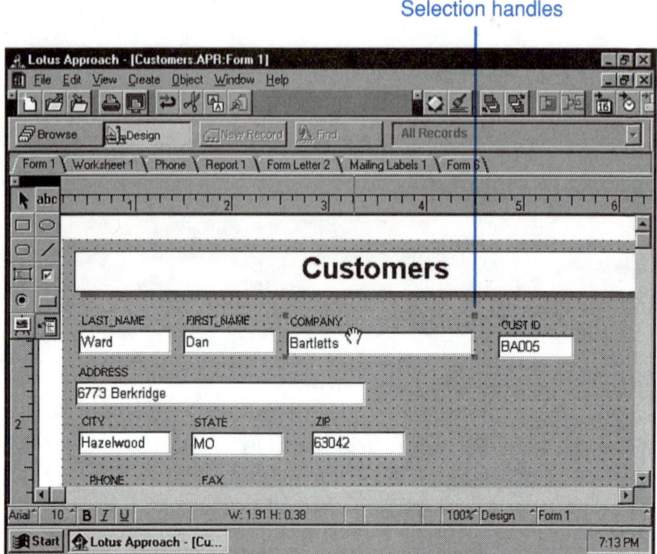

FIGURE 12.4 A selected object.

In this lesson, you learned some skills for working in Design view. In the next lesson, you learn how to use this view to modify the structure of a database.

EDITING A DATABASE STRUCTURE

In this lesson, you will learn how to make some changes to the structure of your database. You'll learn how to add a new field, delete a field, and edit a field.

ADDING A FIELD TO THE DATABASE

After you've used the database a few times, you may decide that you need to make some changes. One common change is to add a field to the database.

When you add a new field to a database, you start by defining it (entering a name, data type, and size). You also must add the field to the form. To do both, you must be in Design view, so start by switching to that view. Then follow these steps:

1. Open the Object menu and select the Add Field command. You see the Add Field dialog box (see Figure 13.1).
2. Click the Field Definition button. You see the Field Definition dialog box (see Figure 13.2).

Use the Tools palette To use the Tools palette to add a field, select the Add Field tool and then draw the new field. Double-click the new field and then click the Field Definition button to define the field.

FIGURE 13.1 Add new fields to the form using this dialog box.

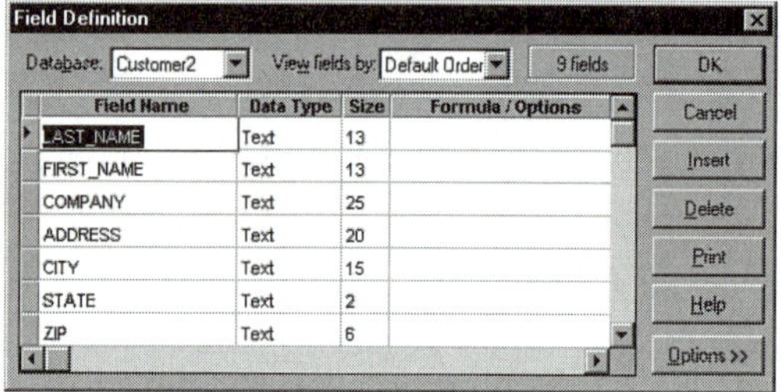

Field Name	Data Type	Size	Formula / Options
LAST_NAME	Text	13	
FIRST_NAME	Text	13	
COMPANY	Text	25	
ADDRESS	Text	20	
CITY	Text	15	
STATE	Text	2	
ZIP	Text	6	

FIGURE 13.2 Use this dialog box to add fields to your database.

3. If you want to insert the new field within the existing ones, select the row and then click the Insert button. Approach adds the new field above the existing field. Or click in the last row in the dialog box.
4. Type the name for the new field and press Tab.
5. Select a data type and press Tab. You can review Lesson 5 for more information on data types.
6. If necessary, enter a field size.
7. Click OK. Approach adds the field to the database, but does not include the field on the form. To add the field to the form, follow the next step.

8. From the Add Field dialog box, drag the field onto the form. Approach adds the field to the form.

Form and database aren't the same When you use the Field Definition dialog box, you are modifying the structure of the database. Keep in mind that the form is simply a view of this database. You can make changes to the database independently of the form and vice versa.

DELETING A FIELD

Just as you can add a field, you can also delete fields that you no longer need. Keep in mind that you can delete a field from the database, and all the data is deleted. If you delete a field from the form, only that view of the database doesn't display the data. The database itself still includes the data.

Follow these steps to remove a field from a database:

1. Display the Field Definition dialog box by double-clicking on the field you want to delete. Approach displays the InfoBox for the selected field (see Figure 13.3).

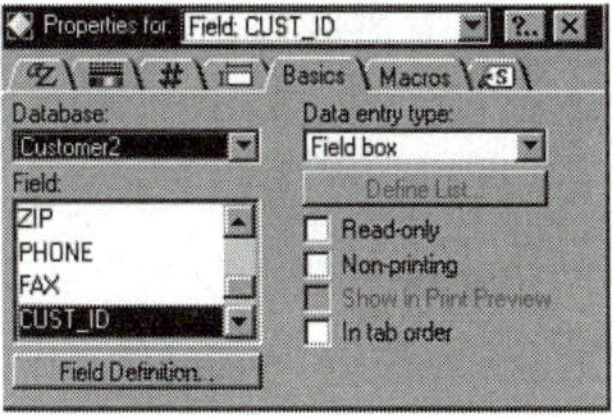

FIGURE 13.3 Use the InfoBox to set properties for the selected field.

2. Click the Field Definition button. In the Field Definition dialog box that appears, the field should be selected.

3. Click the Delete button. Approach reminds you that all data in that field will be deleted and prompts you to confirm the deletion.
4. Click OK.
5. Click the Close button to close the Field Definition dialog box. You can also close the InfoBox by clicking the Close button.

Notice that Approach still includes the field on the form. You can delete the field by following these steps:

1. Click on the field to select it.
2. Click the Delete button. Approach removes the field from the form.

Delete the field from the form You don't have to delete the field from the database; you can simply remove a field from the form and keep it in the database.

EDITING A FIELD

In addition to adding or deleting fields, you can make editing changes to a field. For example, you can change the field name or set a different field size. To make a change, follow these steps:

1. Double-click the field you want to change.
2. Click the Field Definition button.
3. In the Field Definition dialog box, you can do the following:
    - Change the name by typing a new name in the Field Name column.

- Change the data type using the Data Type column.
- Enter a new size in the Size column.

4. When you are finished making changes, click OK.

Be careful! Keep in mind that some changes will affect the data in your database. For example, if you make a field smaller, you may lose some of the data in that field.

Rearranging Fields

The fields are displayed on the default form in the order you entered them. When you look at this form, you may decide that a different arrangement may be visually more appealing. For example, you may want to space the fields out evenly on the form rather than have them one after another in a row.

To move a field, select it and then drag the field to a new position.

Keep in mind that rearranging the fields on the form has no effect on the order you use to enter values in the field. If you want to change the order used for data entry, you need to change the tab order. To do so, follow these steps:

1. Open the View menu and select the Show Tab Order command. Approach displays numbers for each of the fields, indicating the tab order.
2. Edit the numbers so that the fields are in the order you want. When you make a change to one number, all numbers following the change are updated.
3. Click the OK button in the action bar.

In this lesson you learned how to make some changes to the structure of your database and to the default form. The next lesson shows how to use some special types of fields.

Adding Special Types of Fields

In this lesson, you will learn how to add special types of fields to your database.

Creating a Calculated Field

Some fields in a database may not be entries, but the results of a calculation on another field. For example, in an inventory database, you might have fields for Items Ordered, Items Sold, and Items in Stock. Rather than enter each of these, you could create a calculated field for Items in Stock (Items Ordered – Items Sold). Or in an invoice database, you might have fields for Unit Price, Quantity, and Item Total. Rather than enter Item Total, you could create a formula (Unit Price * Quantity).

You can set up a calculated field by following these steps:

1. In Design view, display the Field Definition dialog box.
2. Click in the last row or add the new field within the existing fields by selecting the row and clicking the Insert button. Approach adds the field above the current row.
3. Type a field name and press Tab.
4. For Data Type, select Calculated. Approach expands the dialog box so that you can create the formula (see Figure 14.1).

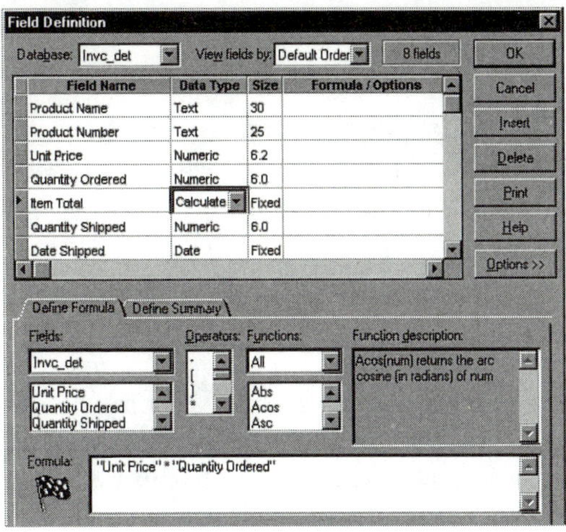

FIGURE 14.1 Use the Define Formula tab to create a formula.

5. Build the formula in the Formula area by selecting fields from the Fields list and operators from the Operators list. You can also type values (for example, Unit Price * .05). Finally, you can select to use a function from the Functions list.

Function A function is a predefined formula. For example, you can use the Sum formula to sum the values in a range.

6. When you are finished creating the formula, click OK. Approach adds the field to the database. You can add the new field to the form by following the next step.

Watch the flag! When you have created a valid formula, the flag no longer has an X on it.

7. Drag the new field from the Add Field dialog box to the form.

Notice that the new field is listed in italics in the Add Field dialog box, reminding you that this field is a calculated field.

ADDING LIST BOXES

To make it as easy as possible to make entries, you may want to be able to select items from a list. For example, suppose you have an order database that includes a field for shipping methods. If you have only a few shipping methods, you could type the method over and over again. Or you could create this field as a list and then select an entry from the list. Using a list box not only makes it easier to make an entry, but this method also ensures accuracy because you (or another user) doesn't have to guess and take the chance of making an inaccurate entry.

You can select from three different styles of lists:

- **Drop-down list** Only the first item in the list is displayed. You can display additional list items by clicking on the down arrow next to the list.
- **Field box & list** This type of list displays a field box (which you can type in) and a list.
- **List box** In this type of list, all the entries are displayed. You can select the entry you want by clicking on the item in the list.

Follow these steps to change an existing field to a list:

1. Double-click on the field you want to change. You see the InfoBox for the selected field (see Figure 14.2).

FIGURE 14.2 Use the InfoBox to modify the selected field.

2. Display the Data Entry Type drop-down list and select the type of list you want to create. Approach displays a list dialog box, as shown in Figure 14.3. (The name of the dialog box varies depending on the type of list you are creating.)

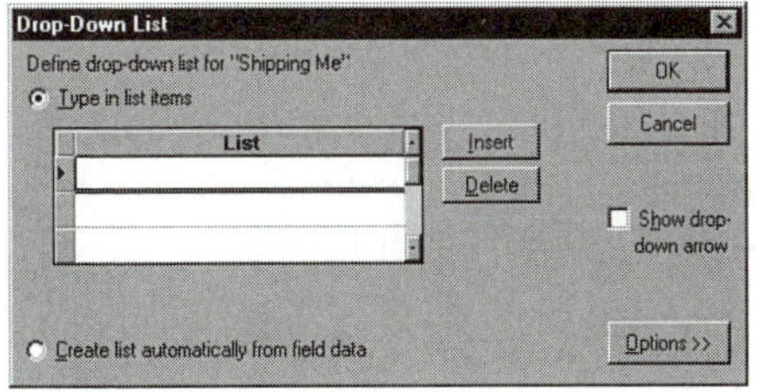

FIGURE 14.3 Create a drop-down list with this dialog box.

3. Select Type in list items and then type the items you want to include. Or select Create list automatically from field data.

4. Click OK. Approach adds the list box.

Be sure to note that you can also add a new field and make it a list box, radio button, or check box field. To do so, add the field, as described in Lesson 13. Then follow the steps, as described in later sections of this lesson.

Adding Radio Buttons

If you have just a few selections, you may want to use radio buttons rather than a list. For example, you could create radio buttons for each of the shipping methods in your order database. To select one of these options when entering data, you simply click the radio button for the entry you want.

Radio button With this type of option, you can select only one of the group. For example, a shipping method can be express or standard, but not both.

Follow these steps to create a radio button:

1. Double-click on the field you want to change. You see the InfoBox for the selected field.
2. Display the Data entry type drop-down list and select Radio buttons. Approach displays the Define Radio Buttons dialog box (see Figure 14.4).

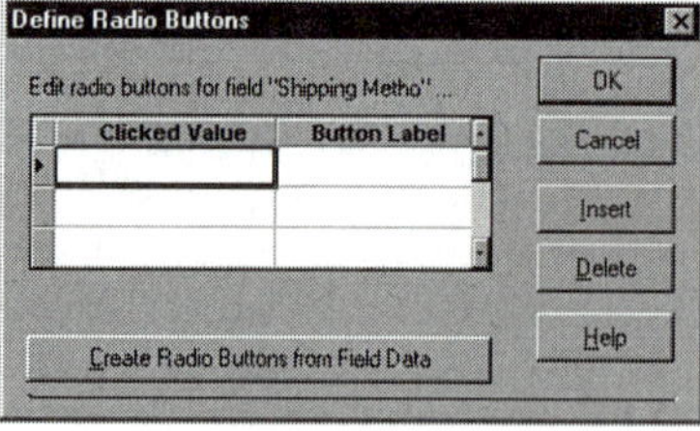

Figure 14.4 Use this dialog box to create radio buttons on your data entry form.

3. Enter the value and label you want to include for each of the buttons. Or select Create Radio Buttons from Field Data to have Approach look at the existing data and create a button for each of the values currently entered.
4. Click OK. Approach adds the radio buttons.

ADDING CHECK BOXES

For some entries, you may want to use a check box. For example, consider the order database again. If you had only two shipping methods, you could set up a check box called Express. If the check box is checked, Approach uses the express shipping method. Otherwise, the entry defaults to standard shipping.

When you set up a check box, you specify the checked value, the unchecked value, and a label for the check box(es). You can create check boxes for text, numeric, date, or Boolean fields. You set up one check box for a field.

Follow these steps to create check boxes:

1. Double-click on the field you want to change. You see the InfoBox for the selected field.
2. Display the Data entry type drop-down list and select Checkboxes. Approach displays the Define Checkbox dialog box (see Figure 14.5).

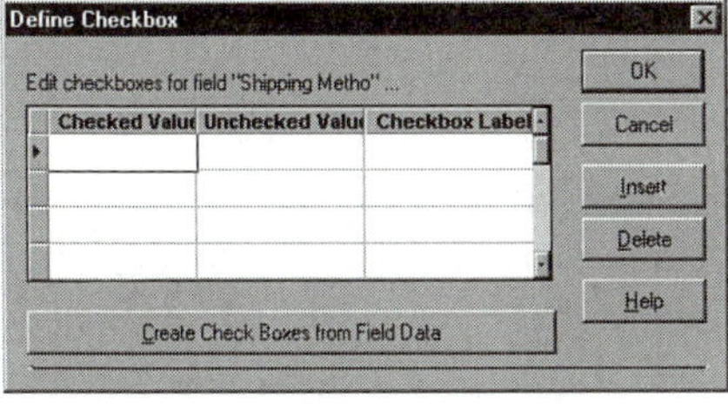

FIGURE 14.5 Use this dialog box to create check boxes.

3. Enter the checked value, unchecked value, and checkbox label for each check box you want to create. Or select Create Check Boxes from Field Data to have Approach look at the existing data and set up the check boxes for you.
4. Click OK. Approach adds the check boxes. Figure 14.6 shows a data entry form with three versions of the same field: a drop-down list box, radio buttons, and check box.

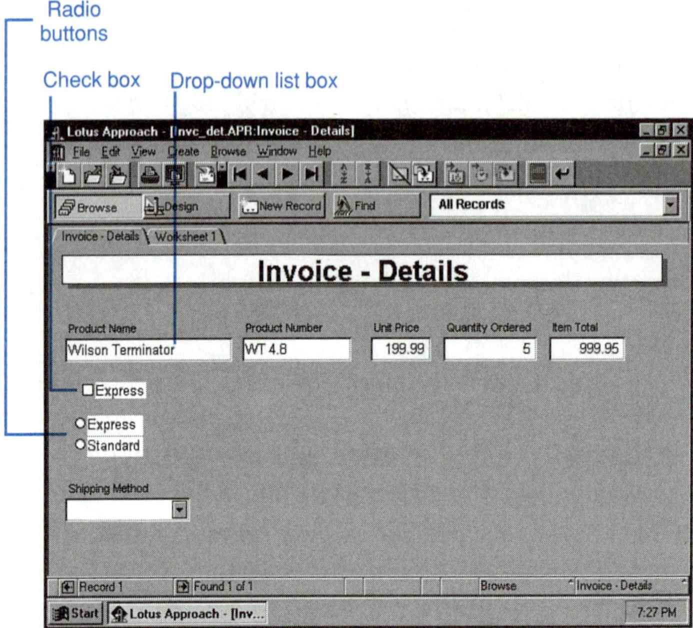

FIGURE 14.6 A data form with a list box, radio buttons, and check box.

In this lesson you learned how to create special types of fields that make entering data easier. The next lesson explains how to make entries automatically and how to validate entries.

Customizing the Form

In this lesson, you will learn how to specify a default entry to make data entry easier. You also learn how to enable Approach to check entries.

Setting a Default Entry

If you find that you are making the same entry over and over, you can set up a default entry that will be used on all new records. When you add a new record, you can simply keep the default. Or if necessary, you can edit or replace the default. When you set up a default, you can select the following options:

Option	Description
Nothing	This is the default. When this is selected, the field is blank.
Previous record	Approach uses the value from the previous record.
Creation date	Approach inserts the current system date in the field.
Creation time	Approach inserts the current system time in the field.
Modification date	Approach inserts the date the record was last modified.
Modification time	Approach inserts the time the record was last modified.
Data	To enter a particular value, select this option and then enter the value you want to use.

continues

continued

Option	Description
Serial number starting at	To enter a serial number, select this option. Then enter a starting number and an increment number.
Creation formula or Modification formula	Approach calculates a formula, and the result will be the default value.

Follow these steps to specify a default value:

1. Double-click on the field and then click the Field Definition button in the InfoBox to display the Field Definition dialog box (make sure you're in Design mode).
2. Click on the Options button. Approach expands the dialog box to display two tabs of options: Default Value and Validation (see Figure 15.1).

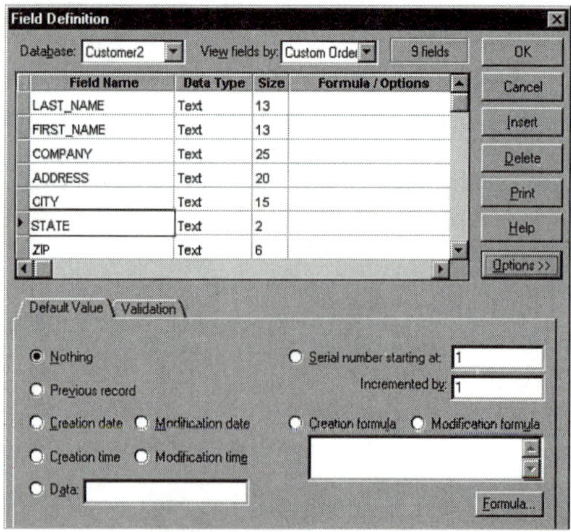

Figure 15.1 Set up default entries on this tab.

3. Select the Default Value tab if it's not already selected, then select the type of default value you want to use (see the preceding table).
4. Click OK.

Set default values To set up default values as you add new fields, define the field, click the Options button, then make your selections for the default.

VALIDATING ENTRIES

Your database is only as good as the data that it contains. If the database includes wrong entries, it won't be of much help to you. To prevent incorrect entries, you have a lot of choices. One of those choices includes having Approach validate entries.

You start by setting the validation option you want. Then, if you (or another user) make an incorrect entry, Approach displays a warning message. Here are the validation options you can select:

OPTION	DESCRIPTION
Unique	Select this option if the field must have a unique value. That is, no other record in the database can contain the same entry in this field.
From and to	To check the entry against a range of values, select this option and then enter the range.
Filled in	If the field must contain an entry, select this option.

continues

continued

OPTION	DESCRIPTION
One of	To check against a list of acceptable entries, select this option. Then type each entry and add it to the list by clicking the Add button. When you set up this type of validation, Approach creates a drop-down list for the field.
Formula is true	To check the entry against a formula, select this option and then create the formula. Creating formulas is covered in Lesson 14.
In field	If the entry must match another value in another field in the database or joined database, select this option and then select the field (and database).

Follow these steps to set validation options:

1. In Design mode, double-click on the field and then click the Field Definition button to display the Field Definition dialog box.
2. Click on the Options button. Approach expands the dialog box to display two tabs of options.
3. Click on the Validation tab. Approach displays the validation options (see Figure 15.2).
4. Select the type of validation (see the preceding table).
5. Click OK.

If you make an incorrect entry during Browse-mode data entry, Approach beeps and displays a warning box (see Figure 15.3). Click OK and then reenter the value.

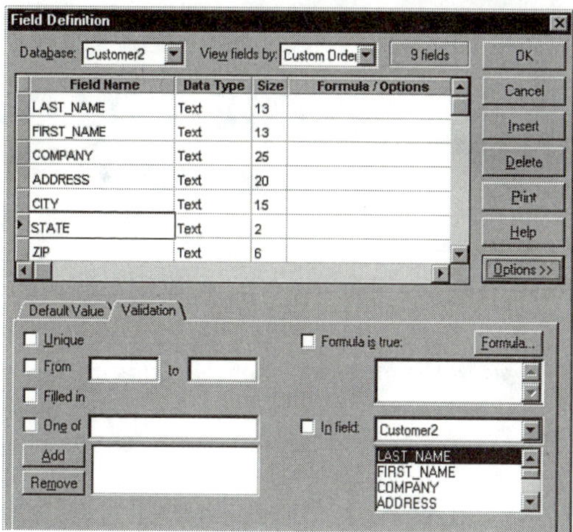

FIGURE 15.2 Have Approach validate entries in the field by using these options.

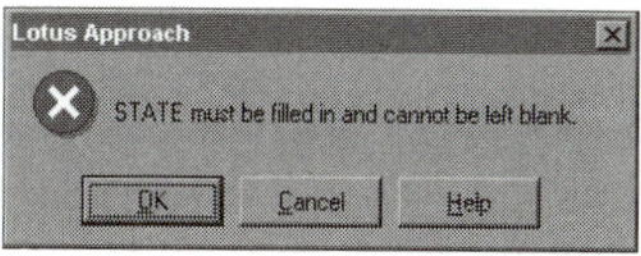

FIGURE 15.3 An error message is displayed if you make an incorrect entry.

In this lesson you have learned some techniques for controlling data entry. The next lesson describes some formatting changes you can make to your data entry form.

LESSON 16

Formatting the Fields in a Form

In this lesson, you will learn how to make some changes to the appearance of the fields and field labels on a form.

Changing the Look of the Data

On a form or report, a field is usually displayed as two parts: the field contents or data and the field label that identifies the field. You can control the appearance of both of these elements.

Formatting Fields

Do you want your field entries to stand out? If so, you can format them so that they appear in boldface or a bigger size. In general, you can select the font, style, size, and color for the field using the InfoBox.

Follow these steps to change the look of your field entries:

1. In Design view, double-click on the field you want to change. Approach displays the InfoBox for the selected field.
2. Click on the Font tab (indicated with the letters az). You see the Font tab options (see Figure 16.1). Be sure that the Data option button is selected.

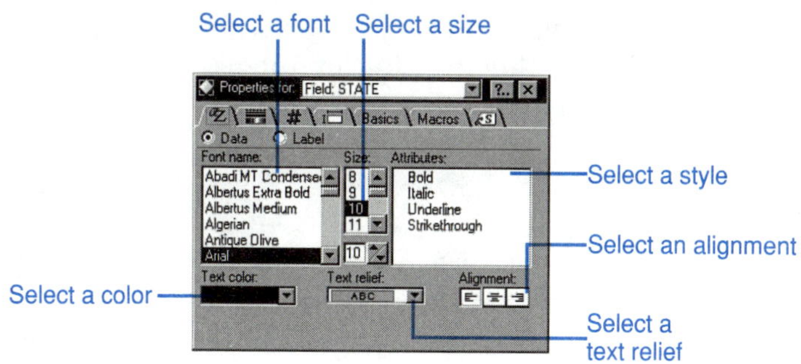

FIGURE 16.1 Select a font for the selected field.

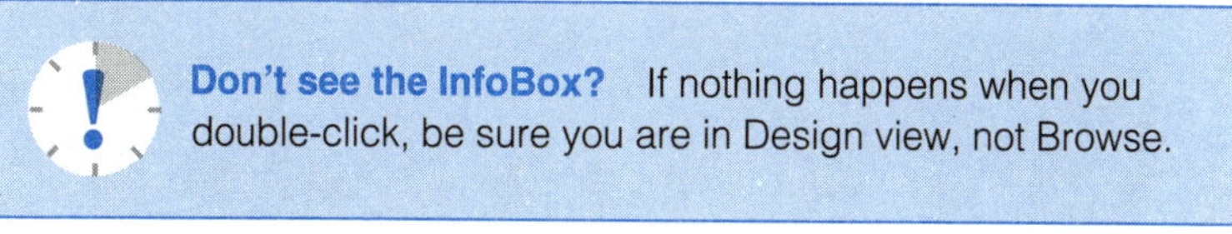

Don't see the InfoBox? If nothing happens when you double-click, be sure you are in Design view, not Browse.

3. Do any of the following:

- To change the font, select the one you want in the Font name list. The fonts that you see listed depend on the fonts you have installed on your system.
- To select a style such as bold or italic, click on the style in the Style/effect list box.
- To use a different size, select the size in the Size list.
- To select a color, display the Text color drop-down list and select a color.
- To select a text relief (how text appears on the background), display the Text relief drop-down list and select a color.
- To change the alignment, click on an Alignment button.

4. When you have finished making changes, close the InfoBox by clicking the Close button. Figure 16.2 shows examples of different format options.

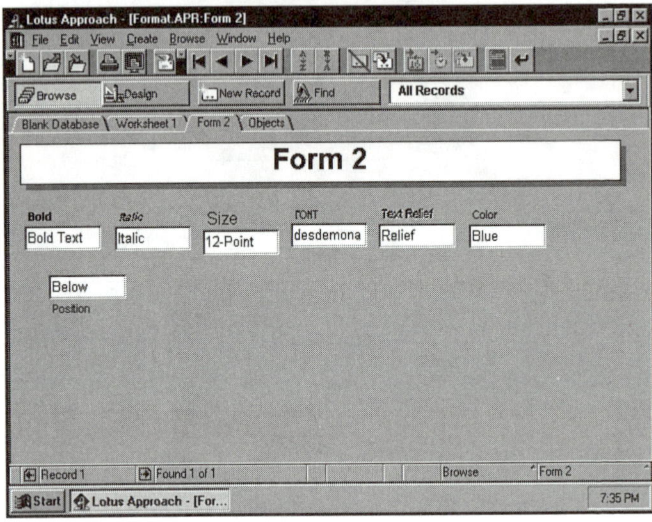

FIGURE 16.2 You can format the field itself and select a font, font size, text relief, or color.

Undo the change If you make a mistake, you can undo the change using the Edit Undo command.

SELECTING A DISPLAY FORMAT FOR THE DATA

Another change you can make to field data is to apply a display format. For instance, if you have a price field in your product database, you may want to format this field so that it appears as currency ($12.99 as opposed to 12.99). You don't have to type the dollar sign or commas (for thousands). Instead, just type the numbers, and Approach will apply the format. You can select a display format for date, time, numeric, and text entries.

To select a display format, follow these steps:

1. In Design view, double-click the field you want to change. You see the InfoBox for the selected field.
2. Click the Format tab (indicated with a # sign). You see the Format tab options (shown in Figure 16.3), which vary depending on the type of field you have selected.

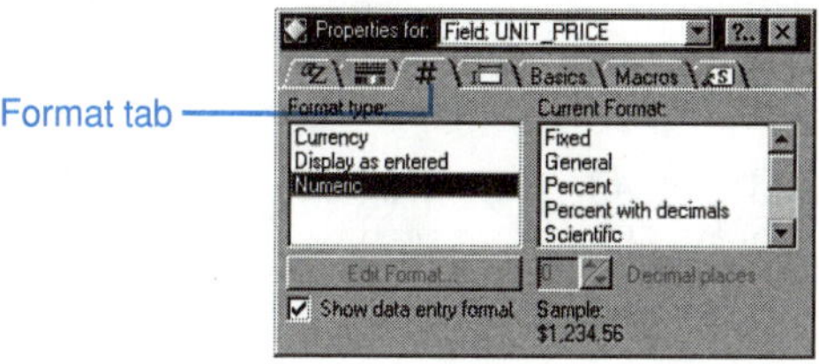

FIGURE 16.3 Use this tab to select a display format.

3. In the Format type list, select a display type.
4. In the Current Format list, select a format. This list will vary depending on the type of format you selected in Step 3. For example, if you select a date format, you will see different styles of dates (04/05, 05-Apr, and so on). If you select a currency format, you'll see different countries.
5. If necessary, make changes to any of the other dialog box options. For instance, when you select some of the numeric formats, you can select the number of decimal places.
6. When you are finished making changes, click the Close button in the InfoBox.

Show the format If you want the format to appear on the form, check the Show Data Entry Format check box.

FORMATTING THE FIELD LABEL

In addition to changing how the data appears on a form, you can also choose how the label (the text that identifies the field) appears. Like formatting a field, you can select the font, style, size, and color for the field label. You can also change the text used for the label and the position.

To format the field label, follow these steps:

1. In Design view, double-click on the field you want to change. Approach displays the InfoBox for the selected field.
2. Click the Font tab.
3. Select the Label option button. Approach displays the Label options, which are similar to those for Data (see Figure 16.4).

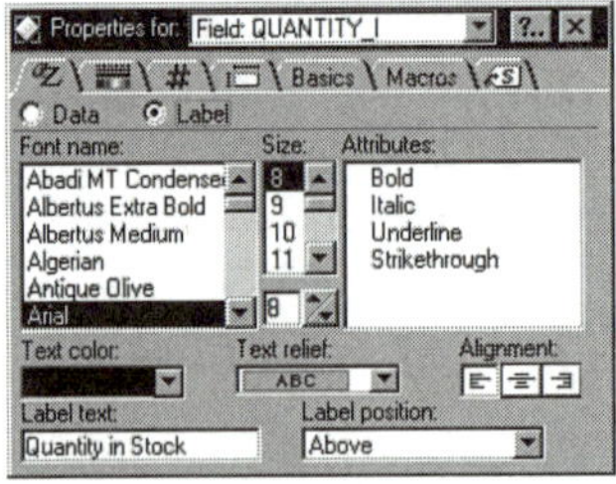

FIGURE 16.4 Choose or change font characteristics for the selected field label.

4. To make a change to the font, do any of the following:
   - To change the font, click on the font you want in the Font name list.

- To select a style such as bold or italic, click on the style in the Attributes list box.
- To use a different size, click on the size in the Size list.
- To select a color, display the Text color drop-down list and select a color.
- To select a text relief, display the Text relief drop-down list and select a color.

5. To select an alignment for the text, click on an alignment button (center, left, or right justified).
6. To use a different name for the label, edit or type a new label in the Label text box.
7. To change the position of the label, display the Label position drop-down list and select a position.

Figure 16.5 shows examples of some formatted labels.

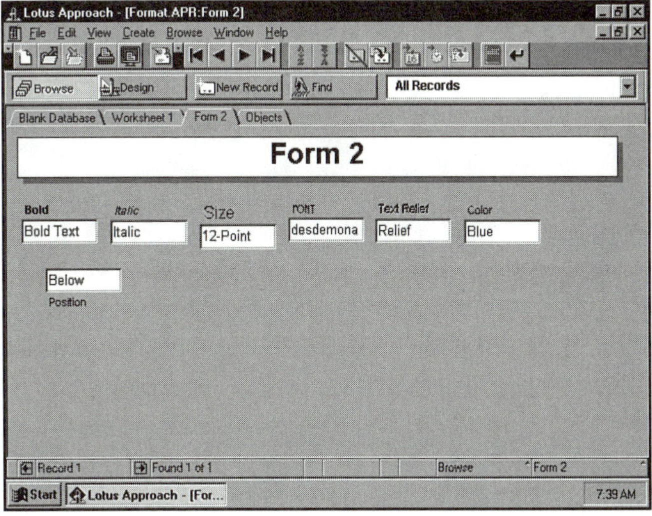

FIGURE 16.5 You can format the field label, select a font, style, color, or position.

In this lesson you learned how to change the appearance of fields and field labels on a form. In the next lesson you will learn some additional appearance changes you can make to the overall form.

Enhancing the Form

Lesson 17

In this lesson, you will learn how to add graphics to a form.

Formatting the Title

At the top of the form, you see a large shadow box that contains the name of the form. This item is a graphic object, called a *text box*, that is added automatically to all new forms. One of the first changes you may want to make is to format the title text box (as shown in Figure 17.1). You can change the text; move or resize the title; and change the font, size, or style of the title.

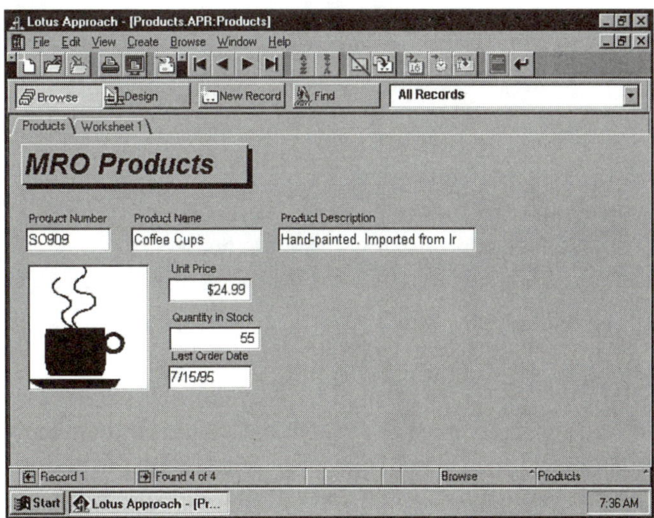

Figure 17.1 The title of this form has been formatted.

To make any changes to the title text box, follow these steps:

1. Switch to Design view.
2. Click on the text box to select it. You should see selection handles around the border.

Note that the icon bar can be used to format the selected object. You can make any of the following changes:

- To make the title bold, italic, or underline, click on the appropriate icon in the icon bar.
- To change the alignment of the title, click on the Center, Left Align, or Right Align icons in the icon bar.
- To display the InfoBox for the object, click on the Change the Properties of the selected object icon in the icon bar. You can then use the InfoBox to set other object properties. This InfoBox works similarly to the one you learned about in the preceding lesson, only the Font tab is missing.
- To make a change to the text itself, double-click the text box.

Quick Delete You can drag across the text to select it and then press Delete to delete it.

DRAWING OBJECTS

In addition to the title text box (which is added automatically), you can add other objects to the form. For example, you may want to call attention to a certain field or divide the form up into sections using lines. Or you may want to add a text box to explain a certain field. You can draw objects on the form using the Tools palette. (To display the Tools palette, open the View menu and select the Show Tools Palette command.)

To draw a line, rectangle, rounded rectangle, or ellipsis on the form, follow these steps:

1. Select the tool you want to use by clicking on it.
2. Move the pointer onto the form where you want to start drawing. The pointer should look like a crosshair.
3. Hold down the mouse button and drag to draw the object. Figure 17.2 shows some objects drawn on the form.

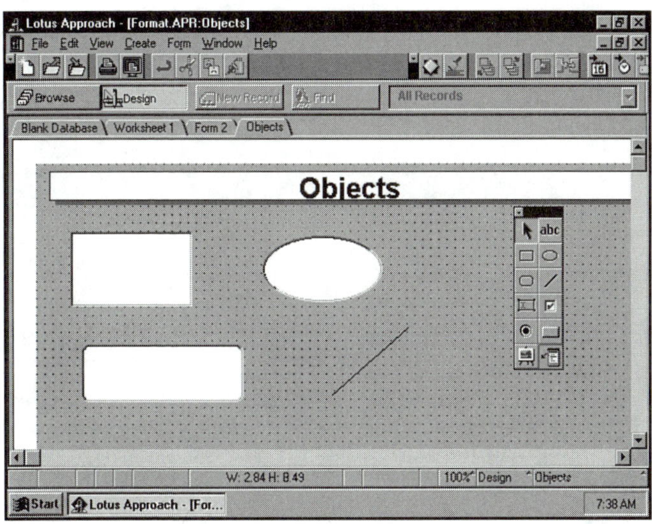

FIGURE 17.2 You can draw objects on the form.

Straight lines, circles, and squares To draw a straight line, a circle, or square, hold down the Shift key as you draw the line, ellipses, or rectangle.

To draw a text box on the form, follow these steps:

1. Click the Text tool.
2. Click where you want to add the text box. Then drag to draw the text box on the form.
3. Type the text. The text wraps automatically within the border of the text box (see Figure 17.3).

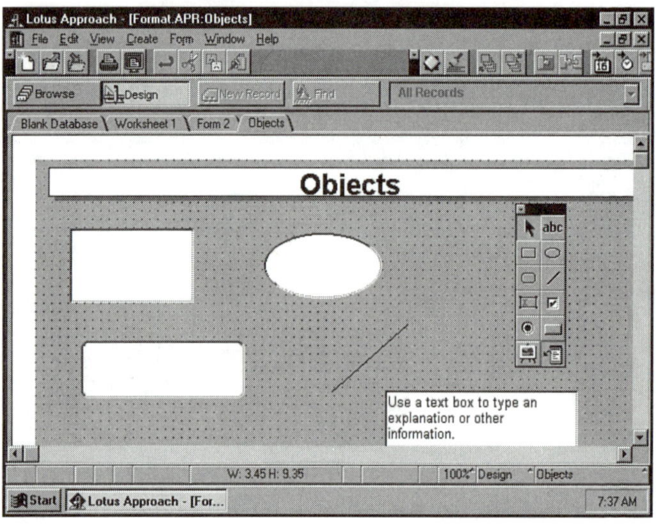

Figure 17.3 You can add a text box to the form.

Notice that you can also use the Tools palette to draw radio buttons, check boxes, or list boxes. For information on making these changes, see Lesson 14.

Pasting a Picture

If you don't want to draw an object, you can use another method to illustrate your form or report: you can paste a picture. For example, you may want to add your company logo or some other clipart image to the form. You can paste the following types of picture files: EPS, TIFF, WMF, BMP, PCX, GIF, TGA, and JPEG.

To paste a picture on the form, follow these steps:

1. Click where you want the upper left corner of the picture to appear.
2. Open the Edit menu and select the Picture command. From the submenu that appears, select Import. You see the Import Picture dialog box (see Figure 17.4).

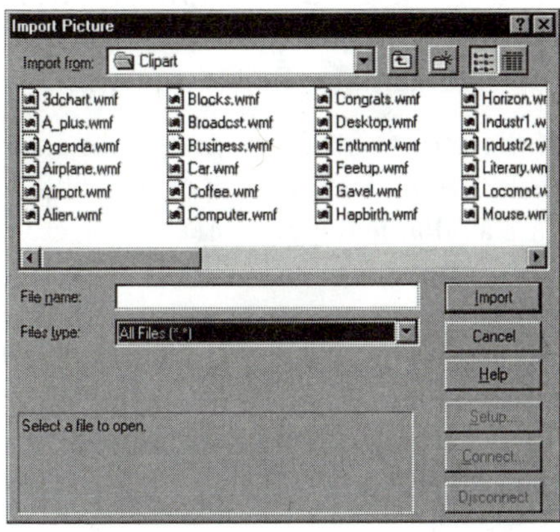

Figure 17.4 Select the picture you want to paste.

3. If necessary, change to the drive and folder where the picture is stored using the folder list or Import from drop-down list.
4. Select the picture you want to import.
5. Click the Import button. Approach adds the picture to the form.

Working with Graphic Objects

When you are adding graphic objects to a form, you will need to do some tinkering to get them drawn and positioned just right. Keep the following tips in mind:

- You can move an object by selecting it and then putting the pointer on a border. Drag the object by its border to a new location.
- To resize an object, select it and then drag one of the selection handles.
- To delete an object, select it and then press Delete.
- To align objects, you can use the grid or rulers. You can also have Approach snap objects to the grid using the Snap to Grid command in the View menu.
- Use the InfoBox to set other properties for an object. To display this InfoBox, double-click on the object. The options that are available depend on the object you have selected.

In this lesson you learned how to enhance the overall appearance of your form by adding and formatting graphic objects. In the next lesson you learn how to create a new form.

LESSON 18

Creating a New Form

In this lesson, you will learn how to create a new form using the Form Assistant.

Selecting a Style and Layout

When you set up a new database, Approach creates a standard form that contains all the fields arranged horizontally. This form can be used to enter and edit data. If you don't like the layout of the form or you don't want to include all the fields from the database, you have two choices. You can modify the default form (using the information covered in Lessons 15–17), or you can create a new form, as covered here.

When you create a new form, you start by selecting a style and layout. Follow these steps:

1. Open the Create menu and select the Form command. You see the Form Assistant dialog box (see Figure 18.1).

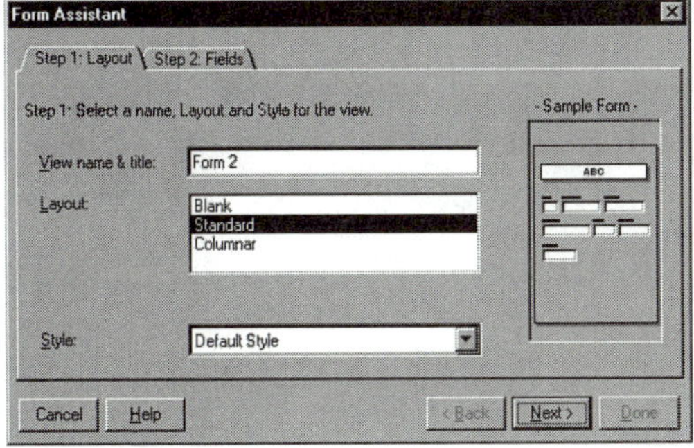

Figure 18.1 Use the Form Assistant to create a new form.

2. In the View name & title text box, type a name for the form. This name will appear in a text box as the title of the form and as the View tab. You can type up to 30 characters.
3. In the Layout list, select the type of layout you want: Blank, Standard (fields are arranged horizontally in rows), or Columnar (fields are arranged vertically in a column).
4. Display the Style drop-down list and select the style you want. Styles control the appearance of the form—such as the colors used, the formatting of the fields, and so on.

Which style or layout should I use? If you aren't sure which style or layout to use, check the Sample Form on the left side of the dialog box for a preview of your selections.

5. Click the Next button.

ADDING FIELDS TO THE FORM

When you click the Next button, you see the Step 2: Fields tab in the Form Assistant dialog box (see Figure 18.2). You can use this tab to select which fields you want to include in the form.

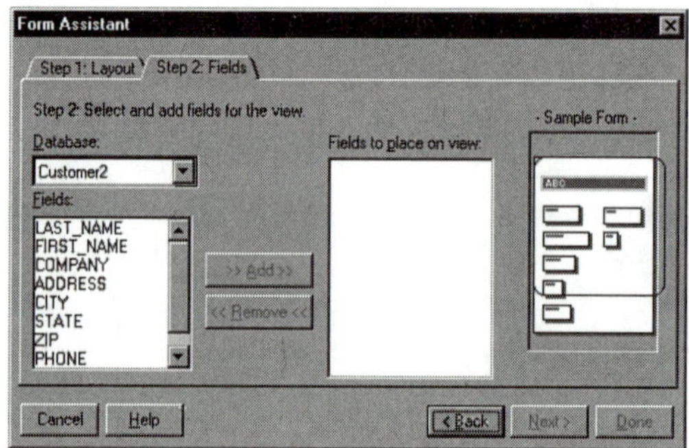

FIGURE 18.2 Select the fields to include in the form.

You have several options when selecting and adding fields:

- To add a single field, select it in the Fields list and then click the Add button or double-click on the field name.
- You can select several fields next to each other by clicking on the first field, holding down the Shift key, and clicking on the last field. The two selected fields and all those in between are selected.
- Hold down the Ctrl key and click to select several fields that aren't next to each other.

When you've added all the fields you want to include, click the Done button. Approach creates the form.

Add a field by mistake? If you add a field by mistake, you can remove it from the list. To do so, click on the field in the Fields To Place on View list and then click the Remove button. Double-clicking will also remove the field.

MODIFYING THE FORM

When you click the Done button in the Form Assistant, Approach displays your new form on-screen (see Figure 18.3).

Keep in mind that you can use and make changes to this form, as follows:

- You can add new fields to the form, move the fields around, or delete fields in Design view. To move a field, select the field and then drag it to a new location. To delete a field, select it and then press the Delete key. To add a new field, display the Add Field dialog box and then drag the field from the Fields in Database list to the form.
- The form is indicated with a form tab. To switch to this form, simply click the tab. To switch to a different form, click on the tab for that form.

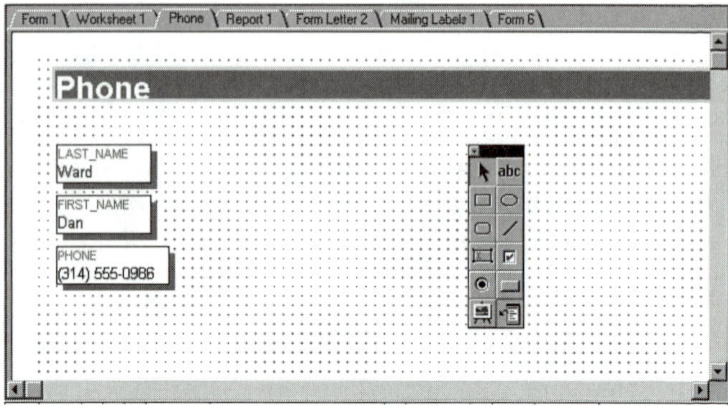

FIGURE 18.3 You can create customized forms.

- To enter data using this form, be sure you are in Browse view. To make changes to the look or structure of the form, change to Design view. (For tips on working in Design view, see Lesson 12.)
- You can change the fields so that they are list boxes, check boxes, or radio buttons rather than entry boxes. See Lesson 14 for information on making these types of changes.
- If you want to make the data (or the field label) stand out, you can change the font used. Formatting fields is the topic of Lesson 16.
- To add objects to the form, display the Tools palette. Lesson 17 covers this topic.

After you make your changes to the form, you will need to save the APR file. Remember that this file stores all the views for a database, and a form is a view. To save the APR file, open the File menu and select the Save Approach File command.

In this lesson you learned how to create a new form. The next lesson covers how to create a different view of the database—a report.

Lesson 19

Creating a Report

In this lesson, you will learn how to create a report using the Report Assistant.

What Is a Report?

A form is useful for working with the data in your database one record at a time—such as when you are editing or adding records. But what about when you want to see a complete list of the data in your database? Do you have to print each record? No, you can create a report instead.

Like a form, *a report* is a view of your database, but in this type of view you can include data from multiple records on a single page. A report enables you to print a phone list of all your employees or a price list of your products. You can also include summary information with a summary panel. This allows you to create a quarterly sales report with the sales total shown in the summary panel.

Panel A report is divided into sections, called *panels*. If you include summary information, Approach adds a summary panel. If you include data from more than one database, you can create repeating panels. See Lesson 27 for more information on repeating panels and joined databases.

To help you create a report, Approach includes the Report Assistant (see Figure 19.1), which leads you step-by-step through the process.

SELECTING A STYLE AND LAYOUT

The first step in creating a new report is to enter the name and select a style and layout. The name appears at the top of the report and on the view tab for the report. The style controls formatting options such as the text attributes for the fields. As for layout, you can select blank, standard, columnar, and summary. These layouts differ in how the record and fields are arranged:

- In a standard layout, the database fields are displayed in one continuous column, and each field is in its own row.
- In a columnar layout, the fields are displayed in the column, and each record is in its own field.
- A blank report is like starting from scratch.

Summary reports are covered later in this lesson.

You make your selections for the name, style, and layout in the Report Assistant. Follow these steps to get started:

1. Open the Create menu and select the Report command. You see the Report Assistant dialog box (see Figure 19.1).

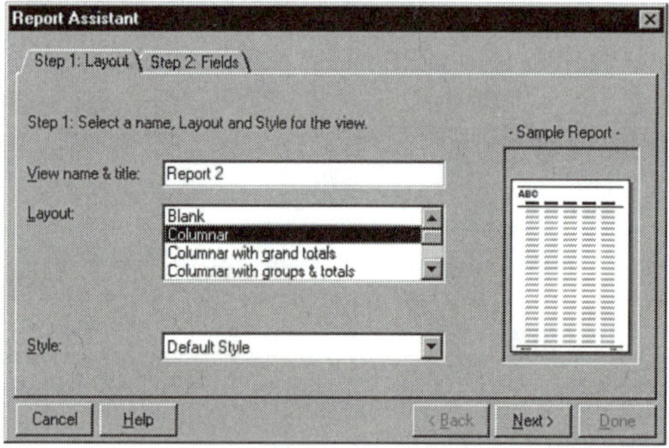

FIGURE 19.1 Use the Report Assistant to create a new report.

2. In the View name & title text box, type a name for the report. You can type up to 30 characters.

3. In the Layout list, select a layout for the report.
4. Display the Style drop-down list and select the style you want. Styles control the formatting of the report (how fields appear, for instance).

What style or layout should I use? If you aren't sure which style or layout to use, check the Sample Report on the right side of the dialog box. You can get a preview of your selections in this area.

Make a mistake? If you make a mistake or change your mind, you can click on the Back button to go back to the preceding step.

5. Click the Next button.

ADDING FIELDS

When you click the Next button, you see the Step 2: Fields tab in the Report Assistant dialog box (see Figure 19.2). You can use this tab to select which fields you want to include in the report.

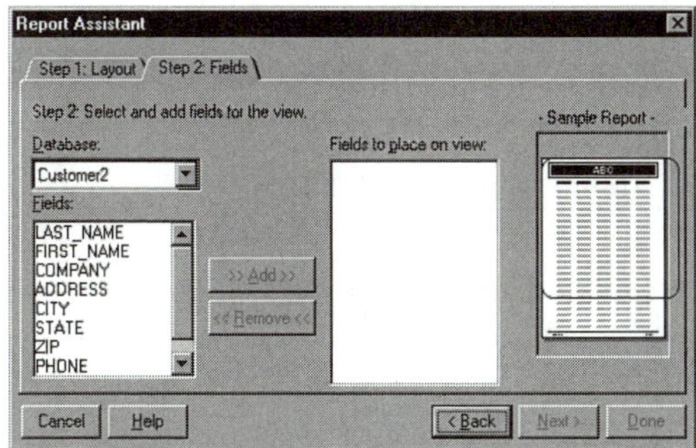

FIGURE 19.2 Select the fields to include in the report.

You have several options when adding fields:

- To add a field, select it in the Fields list and then click the Add button or double-click the field name.
- To select fields that are next to each other, click on the first field and then hold down the Shift key and click on the last field.
- To select fields that aren't next to each other, hold down the Ctrl key and click on each field you want to select.

To add the selected fields to the view, click the Add button. When you've added all the fields you want to include, click the Done button. Approach creates the report (see Figure 19.3).

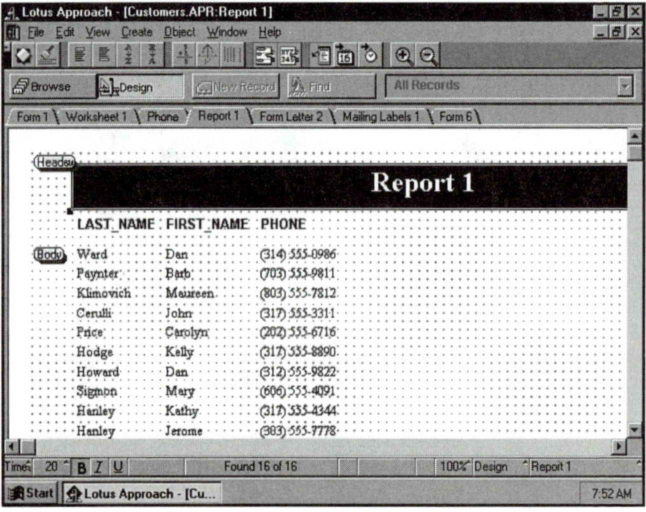

FIGURE 19.3 An example of a report.

If the report isn't exactly how you want it, you can make formatting changes (as covered in the next lesson). Once the report is how you want it, you can print it, as covered in Lesson 21.

Creating a Summary Report

You may want to create a report to calculate and display some summary information. For example, if you used a database to track your sales reps' sales totals, you could create a report that summarized their quarterly sales. In a summary report, you select the field that groups the records, the calculation you want performed, and the field to use for the calculation. Taking the sales rep example, you would want to group the report by sales reps. Each sales rep would have his or her own section of the report. Select Sum for the calculation to perform and then select Sales Total field for the field to calculate.

Follow these steps to create a summary report:

1. Open the Create menu and select the Report command. You see the Report Assistant.
2. In the View name & title text box, type a name for the report, up to 30 characters.
3. In the Layout list, select one of the group layouts.
4. Display the Style drop-down list and select the style you want.
5. Click the Next button. You see the Step 2 tab of the Report Assistant.
6. Add the fields you want to include in the report. Then click the Next button. Approach displays the Step 3 tab of the Report Assistant (see Figure 19.4).
7. To group the fields, select the field from the Fields list and then click the Add button. You can select more than one group field. Then click the Next button. Approach displays the Step 4 tab of the Report Assistant (see Figure 19.5).

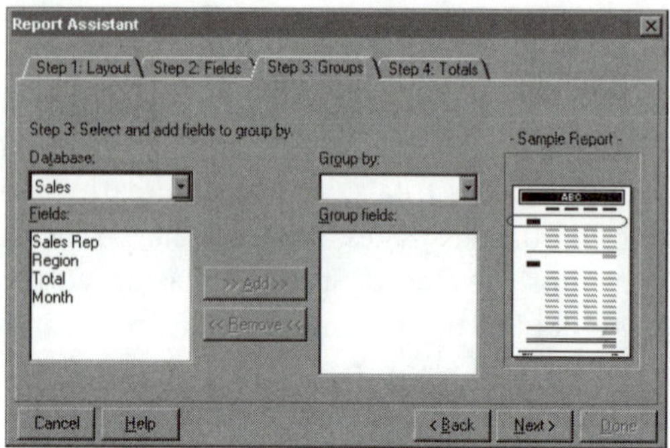

FIGURE 19.4 Use this tab to select the fields to group by.

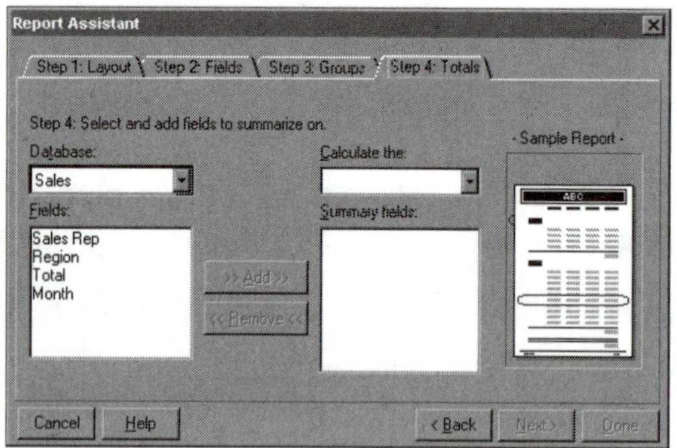

FIGURE 19.5 Select the fields to summarize.

8. To summarize the fields, select the field in the Fields list and then click the Add button.
9. To perform a calculation, display the Calculate the drop-down list and select a calculation function.
10. Click the Done button. Approach creates the report, as shown in Figure 19.6.

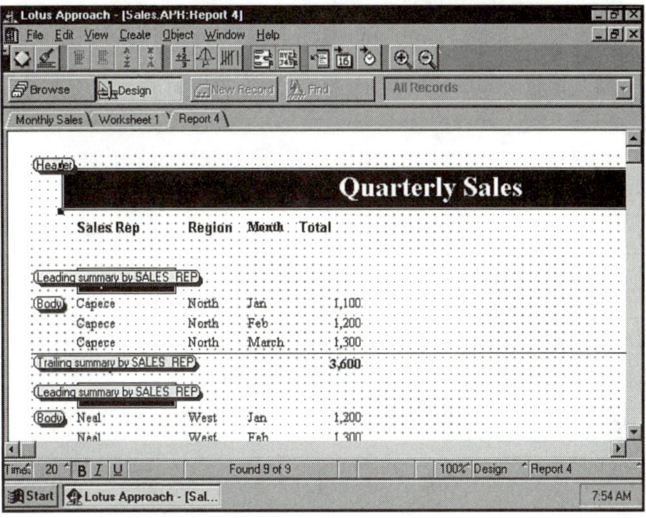

FIGURE 19.6 A summary report can calculate totals and group data.

SAVING THE REPORT

If you want to use the report again, you have to save this view (which is saved with the APR file). If you exit without saving, Approach will remind you, but it's a good idea to get into the habit of saving anyway. To save the Approach file, open the File menu and select the Save Approach File command.

In this lesson you learned how to create a report. The next lesson covers how to make formatting changes to this report.

Formatting a Report

In this lesson, you will learn how to make some formatting changes to a report.

Understanding the Parts of a Report

When you create a report, the Report Assistant takes your selections and creates a finished report. If you like the results, you can simply preview and then print the report (covered in the next lesson). If you want to make some changes, you can do so in Design view.

In Design view, you can see how the report is set up. Each section (called a *panel*) has a name, which is displayed next to the panel. Depending on the type of report, you may have the following panels: Panel, Description, or Header. Figure 20.1 shows the Header panel label being displayed.

Typical panel labels include the following:

Header	The header displays the report name and any column headings. This information is repeated on each page of the report. You can also include other information in this panel (the date, the page number, and so on).
Body	The main part of the report is the body, which contains the information from the records in your database.

Footer	The footer appears at the bottom of the report and usually includes the date by default. You can also include other information in the footer.
Summary panels	If you created a summary report, you may have several summary panels.

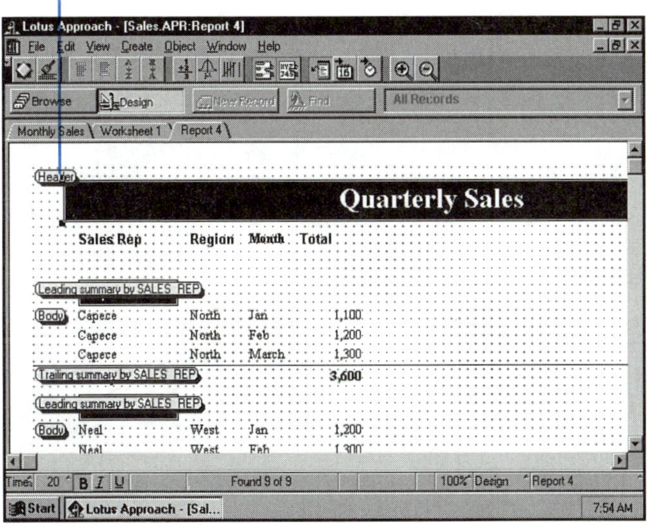

FIGURE 20.1 Report panel names appear along the left edge of the window.

Don't see the panel labels? Panel labels appear only in Design view, so first be sure you are there. If you are in Design view and still don't see the labels, open the View menu and select the Show Panel Labels command to display them.

FORMATTING A REPORT PANEL

One of the changes you may want to make is to enhance the look of your panels. For example, you may want more space between the panels, or you may want to use a different style border. You can make these changes using the InfoBox for the panel.

When you want to modify a panel, you start by selecting it. You can select the panel by doing any of the following:

- clicking a panel border
- clicking within the panel
- clicking on the panel label

In Figure 20.2, the box indicates that the Header panel is selected. Note that the menu bar now includes a menu named Panel.

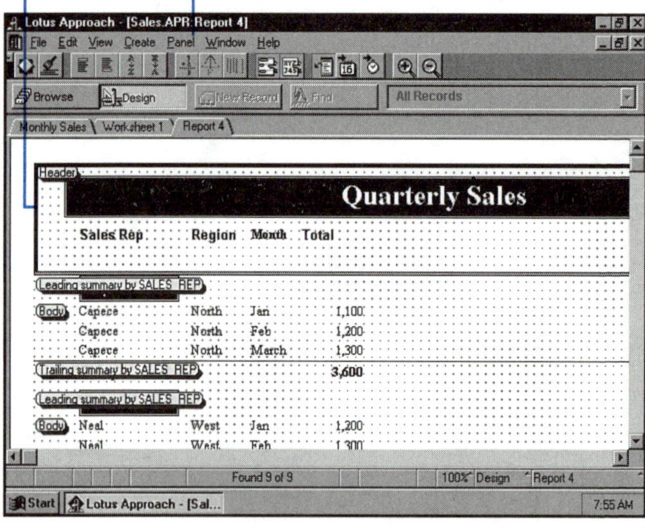

FIGURE 20.2 Select the panel you want to format.

Once the panel is selected, you can make the following changes:

- To resize the panel, drag one of the borders.

- To delete a panel from the report, select it and then press the Delete key.
- To move a panel, drag it to a new location. You can only drag summary panels; you can't move the Header, Body, or Footer panels.
- To format the panel (change the lines between panels, for instance), double-click on the panel. Or open the Panel menu and select the Panel Properties command. Make any changes in the InfoBox that appears. This InfoBox, similar to the one covered in Lesson 16, includes tabs for changing the font, modifying the borders, using display formats, and so on.

FORMATTING THE COLUMNS

If panels divide the report into sections horizontally, columns divide the report vertically. Like panels, you can format the columns in your report. For instance, you may want to make a column wider, or you may want to apply a display format to the entries in a column.

To change the column size, click on the column to select it and then simply drag the column border to widen or narrow the column.

To format the column, follow these steps:

1. Double-click the column, or open the Column menu and select the Column Properties command. You see the InfoBox, which includes tabs for formatting columns (see Figure 20.3).
2. The InfoBox includes tabs similar to those for formatting fields. Select the tab you want and make your changes.
3. Click the Close button.

You can find more information on the InfoBox in Lesson 16.

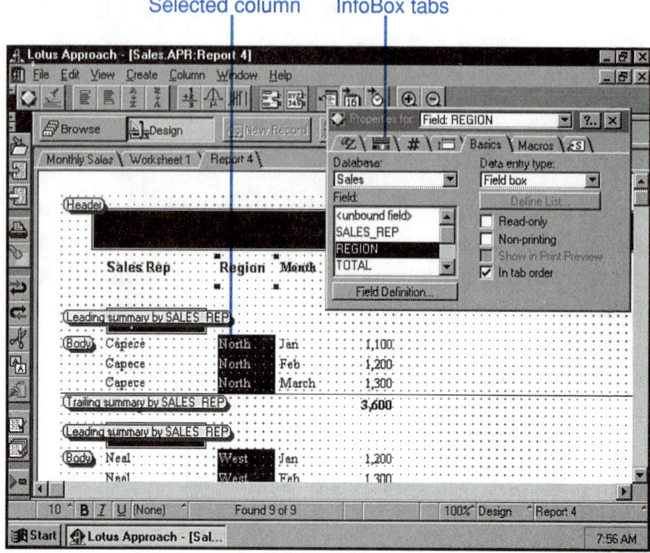

FIGURE 20.3 Use this InfoBox to format the columns in your report.

WORKING WITH HEADERS, FOOTERS, AND TITLE PAGES

By default, Approach includes a header and footer. You can add information to these panels, or you can turn them off. In addition, you can add a title page.

To turn on or off the header, footer, or title page, open the Panel menu (the menu name may vary depending on what you have selected). Then select the Add Header, Add Footer, or Add Title Page command. When there's a checkmark next to the command, the panel is included in the report. You can select the command again to remove the checkmark and the panel.

To add text to the header, footer, or title page:

1. Select the panel where you want to place the text.
2. Then use the Tools palette to draw a text box and type the text you want to include. (You can also draw objects).

3. To include the date, time, or page number, you can open the Insert menu and select Today's Date, Current Time, or Page Number. Approach adds a text box that you can move to any place within the panel.

CHANGING THE REPORT MARGINS

By default, Approach uses .25-inch margins on all sides of the report. If you prefer a different margin, you can make a change. Follow these steps:

1. Click on the report, but not within a panel. This step selects the report.
2. Open the Report menu and select the Report Properties command. You see the InfoBox for the report.
3. Click on the Margins tab. You see the Margins tab options (see Figure 20.4).

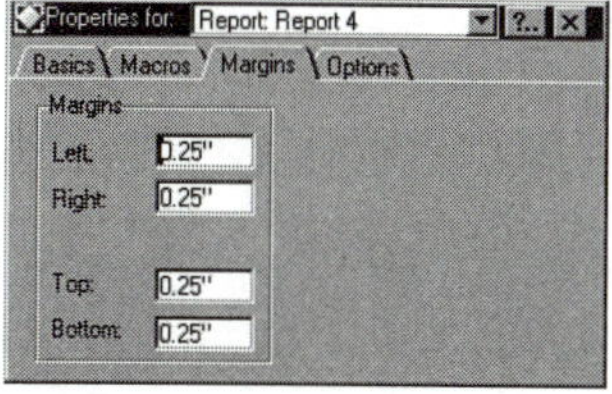

FIGURE 20.4 Use this tab to enter margins for the report.

4. Enter the margins you want for the Left, Right, Top, and Bottom margins. Then click the Close button.

In this lesson you learned about some formatting changes you can make to a report. Turn to the next lesson for information on previewing and printing a report.

Previewing and Printing

In this lesson, you will learn how to set up your printer, preview a view, and then print a view.

Understanding What You Can Print

Remember that Approach includes several types of views, including forms and reports. You can print each of these views. If you print a form, you print each record on a separate page. Any formatting (display formats, objects, printed, and so on) included on the form is printed.

If you print a report, Approach prints all the records that will fit on one page and then prints another page until the report is complete. Depending on the report format, the report may include a title page, headers and footers, and summary sections. See Lessons 19 and 20 for information on creating and formatting reports.

Likewise, you can print a worksheet, crosstab, or chart (charts are covered in Lesson 26). A worksheet is a different view of your data in which the records are arranged in rows. Worksheets are covered in Lesson 24. A crosstab is a special type of worksheet used to summarize data. See Lesson 25 for more information on crosstabs.

Setting Up Your Printer

Windows 95 takes care of setting up your printer. If the printer is hooked up and online, you can print simply by using the Print command.

If you want to check or make changes to your printer setup, follow these steps:

1. Open the File menu and select the Print command. Approach displays the Print dialog box.
2. Click on the Properties button to display the Print Setup dialog box (see Figure 21.1).

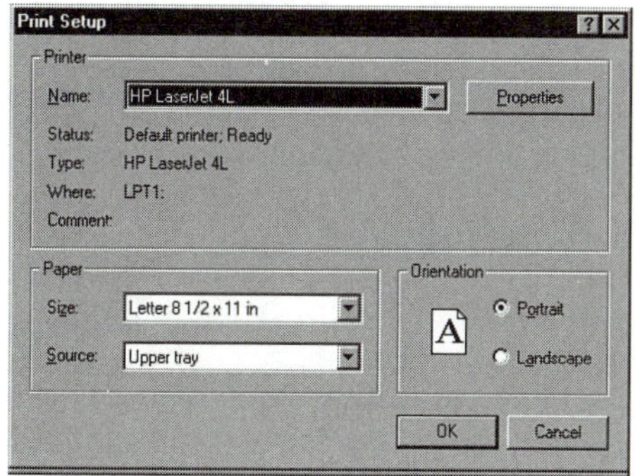

FIGURE 21.1 Use this dialog box to set up your printer.

Printer not in list? If your printer isn't listed, you have not set it up in Windows. You need to do so using the Add Printer wizard.

3. Select the printer you want to set up from the Name drop-down list.
4. Select Portrait or Landscape for the orientation. Portrait prints down the long side of the page; landscape prints across the long side.
5. To change the paper size, display the Size drop-down list and select the size you want.

6. To change the paper source, display the Source drop-down list and select the bin or tray for the paper.
7. Click OK.

Be careful! Keep in mind that the changes you make here will affect all print jobs. If you just want to change an individual print job, use the Page Setup command instead (see next section).

SETTING UP THE PAGE

In some cases, you will want to print a certain view and change the printer settings. Rather than change them for all print jobs, you can change them for the individual view by following these steps:

1. Open the File menu and select the Page Setup command. Approach displays the Page Setup dialog box (see Figure 21.2).

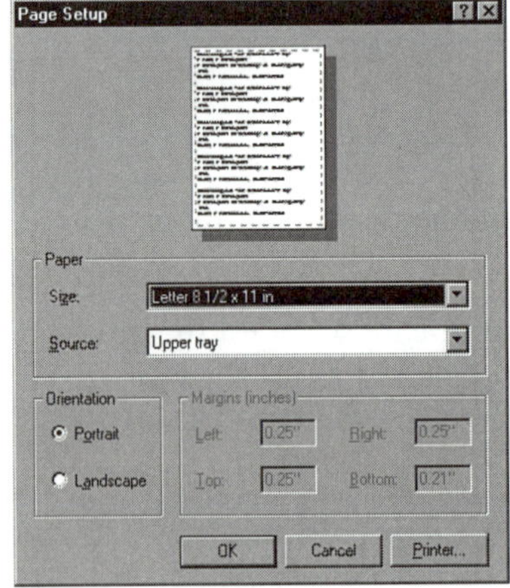

FIGURE 21.2 Use this dialog box to tailor your printer settings.

2. Select Portrait or Landscape for the orientation.
3. To change the paper size, display the Size drop-down list and select the size you want.
4. To change the paper source, display the Source drop-down list and select the bin or tray for the paper.
5. Click OK.

PREVIEWING A VIEW

Before you print, you may want to get an idea of how the view will look when printed. You can check this with a preview and then make any changes before printing. Doing so may save you some time and paper.

To preview, follow these steps:

1. Select the view you want to preview. For instance, if you want to preview a form, click on the form's tab.
2. Open the File menu and select the Print Preview command or click the Preview icon. Approach displays a preview. In Figure 21.3, you see a preview of a report.

Zoom in and out You can use the left mouse button to enlarge, the right one to zoom out again on the view, or by opening the View menu and selecting the Zoom In or Zoom Out commands.

In preview, you can display additional pages. (If you are printing a form view, each record will print on a separate page. For reports, the pages will depend on how many records fit on one page.) You cannot edit the data in preview.

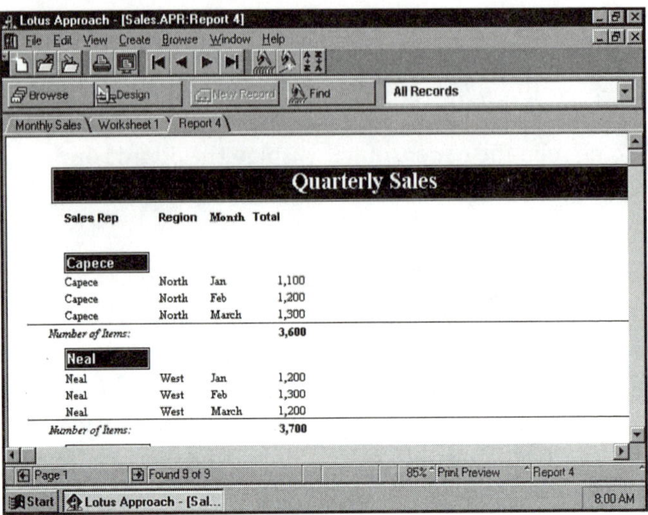

FIGURE 21.3 Preview a view before you print.

PRINTING

After you've previewed the view, you can print. Follow these steps:

1. Select the view you want to print by clicking on the tab for the view.
2. Open the File menu and select the Print command (or click the Print button). Approach displays the Print dialog box (see Figure 21.4).
3. If you want to print just a range of pages, select Pages and then enter the page numbers in the from and to text boxes. To print just the current page, select Current Page.
4. To print more than one copy, enter the number to print in the Copies text box. If you select more than one copy, select whether to collate the copies (optional).
5. Click OK. Approach prints the view.

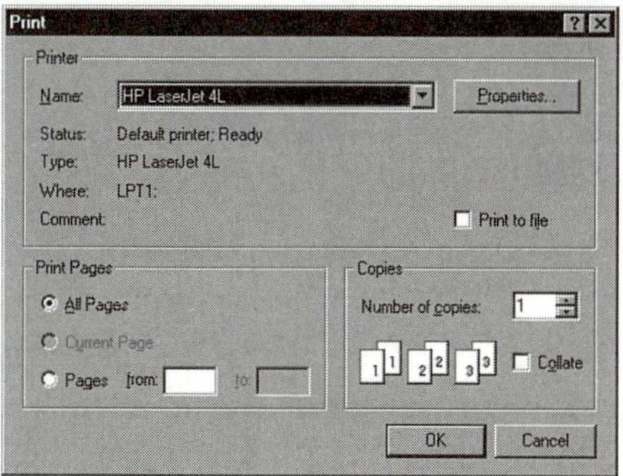

FIGURE 21.4 Select the range to print and the number of copies in the Print dialog box.

PRINTING TIPS

When you are printing a view, keep in mind the following tips:

- If you are printing a form, you may want to sort the records so that they are in an appropriate order. Sorting records is covered in Lesson 11.
- If you are printing a form and don't want to include all the records in your database, you can create a find set. Group the records you want to print using the Find command, as covered in Lesson 10. Then print.
- You can change the appearance of the form by formatting the fields (covered in Lesson 16).
- You can illustrate a report or form by drawing objects or pasting clip art. Lesson 17 covers these skills.

In this lesson, you learned how to print the data in your database. The next lesson covers how to create another type of printed document—a form letter.

Lesson 22 Creating Form Letters

In this lesson, you'll learn how to create a form letter.

What Is a Form Letter?

If you looked at how people use databases, you would probably find that the majority of users have at least one database that is a list of names and addresses. That list may be of clients, customers, vendors, friends, contacts, or any other group of people. A database in its simplest form can be a sort of Rolodex.

Not only is an address list a common type of database, but it is common for users to want to send something to the people in the database. To make it easy to send materials to the names in an address database, Approach includes a special type of view called a *form letter*. With this type of view, you can include fields from the database (such as name, address, city, and so on) and text that you type (such as a letter). When you print the form letter, Approach creates a personalized letter for each person in the database.

To help you create this type of view, Approach includes a Form Letter Assistant, which leads you step by step through the process.

Selecting a Layout

The first step in creating a form letter is to start the Form Letter Assistant and select the style and layout. Notice that this first step is similar to the first step for creating a new form or report. Follow these steps:

1. Open the Create menu and select the Form Letter command. You see the Form Letter Assistant (see Figure 22.1).

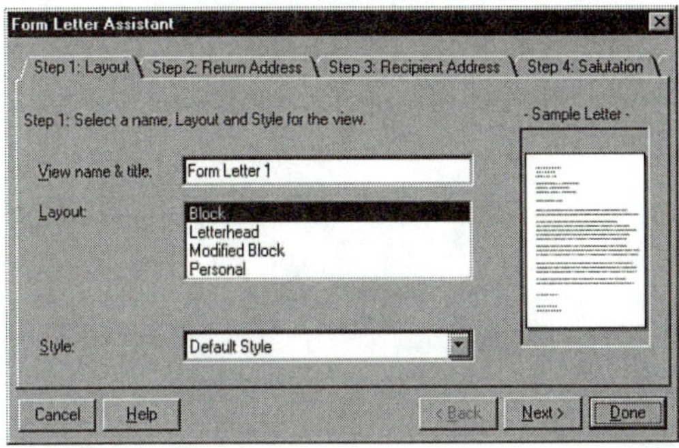

FIGURE 22.1 The Form Letter Assistant, with the Step 1 tab displayed.

2. In the View name & title text box, type a name for the form letter. You can type up to 30 characters.
3. In the Layout list, select a layout for the form letter. You can select a block letter, letterhead, modified block, or personal. The difference is in the placement of the addresses.

Not sure about the style or layout? If you aren't sure which style or layout to use, check the Sample Report in the dialog box. You can get a preview of your selections in this area.

4. Display the Style drop-down list and select the style you want. Styles control the formatting of the form letter (which font is used).
5. Click the Next button.

ENTERING THE RETURN ADDRESS

When you click the Next button, you see the Step 2 tab (see Figure 22.2). On this tab, type your return address or select None if you don't want to include your address (or if it is already included on the envelope). Then click the Next button.

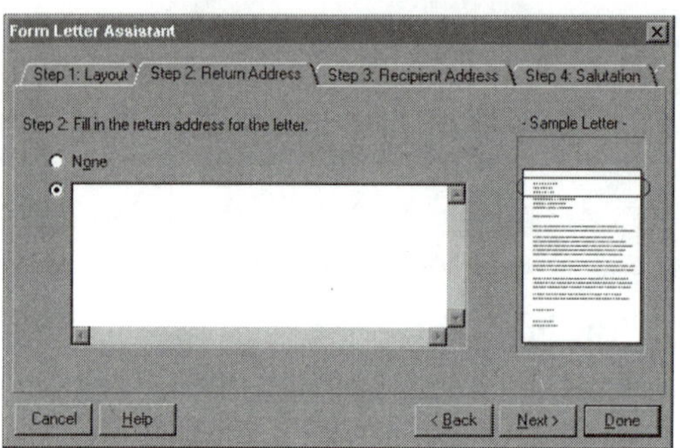

FIGURE 22.2 Type your return address at the Step 2 tab.

CREATING THE RECIPIENT'S ADDRESS

At the Step 3 tab (see Figure 22.3), you enter the addresses for the recipients. Rather than type this information, you select the fields to include for the address. When you print the form letters, Approach will use the data from each field to create a personalized letter.

Follow these steps to set up the inside address:

1. To select the layout (number of address lines), display the Address layout drop-down list and select the one you want. Notice that Approach displays blanks for each area of a typical address and that the first area is selected in the Fields for the address list.

2. In the Fields list, click on the field you want to include in the first address slot. Then click the Add button. Approach adds the field and moves to the next slot.

3. Continue completing the slots with fields until you add all the fields you want to include. To skip a slot, simply click on the next one. To remove a field, click on it and then click on the Remove button.

4. When you are finished adding fields, click on the Next button.

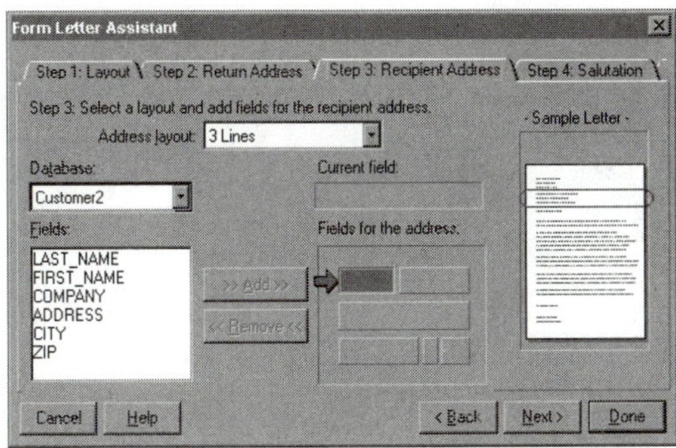

FIGURE 22.3 Create the recipient's address.

TYPING THE SALUTATION

Most letters include a greeting or salutation. Follow these steps to enter the greeting:

1. In the Step 4 tab, enter the text for the greeting (see Figure 22.4). The default is **Dear**, but you can replace this greeting with something else.

2. Select the field or fields to use. For example, you can select FIRST_NAME (Dear John) or FIRST_NAME and LAST_NAME (Dear John Doe).

3. After you type the salutation, click the Next button.

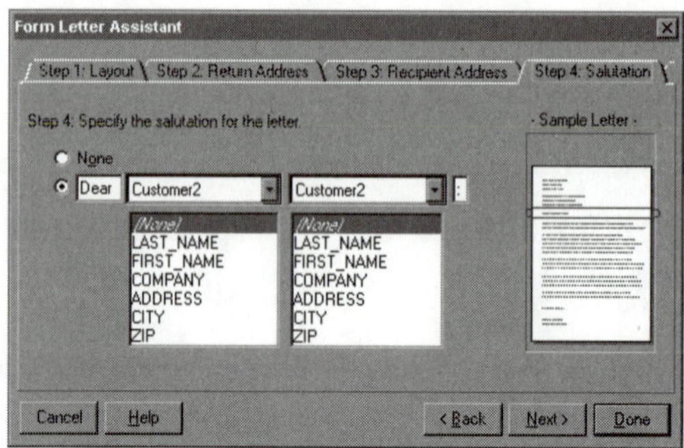

FIGURE 22.4 Type the greeting and select which fields to include.

TYPING THE CLOSE

For Step 5, simply type the closing you want to include for the letter (see Figure 22.5). You can keep the traditional **Sincerely yours** and add your name, or you can replace the default closing with your own. When you complete the closing, click the Next button.

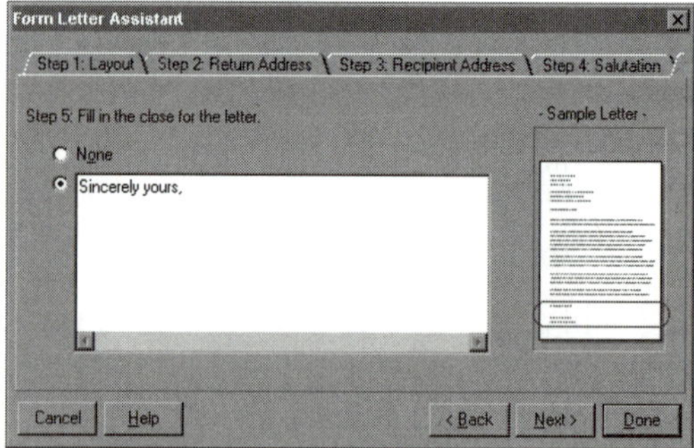

FIGURE 22.5 Type the closing.

Create envelopes You can have Approach set up envelopes for you as part of the form letter in Step 6. You can skip the Step 6 tab for now. You will learn how to set up envelopes in the next lesson.

TYPING THE FORM LETTER

After you set up the form letter, Approach displays the letter onscreen (see Figure 22.6). Fields appear in brackets. To create the body of the letter, click where you want to add text and then type. You can add text to any part of the form letter.

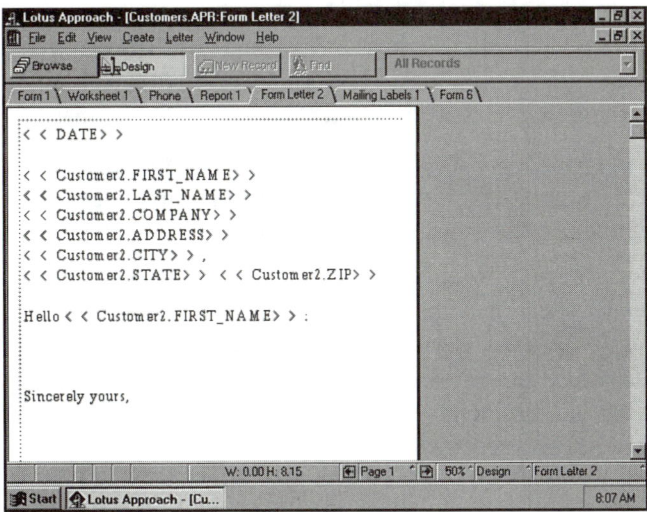

FIGURE 22.6 Type the letter.

When you complete the letter, save the Approach file. Then you can preview and print the form letter, as described in Lesson 21.

This lesson explained how to create a form letter. The next lesson shows how to create mailing labels and envelopes.

Creating Mailing Labels and Envelopes

In this lesson, you will learn how to create mailing labels and envelopes using the addresses in a database.

Creating Envelopes

As you learned in the last lesson, you may want to send mail to the people in your database. The last lesson described how to create the letter; to mail that letter, you'll need envelopes.

You can create envelopes as part of the form-letter process. (In the Form Letter Assistant, there's a tab for setting up envelopes.) Or you can set up the envelopes separately, as covered here.

Keep in mind that to print envelopes, your printer must be able to handle envelopes. Depending on the type of printer you have, you may have a special tray for envelopes, or you may have to manually feed the envelopes. Approach enables you to select from one of several different standard envelope sizes, so you don't have to worry about aligning the address on the envelope.

Follow these steps to set up envelopes:

1. Open the Create menu and select the Envelopes command. Approach displays the Envelope Assistant (see Figure 23.1).
2. In the View name & title text box, type a name for this view, up to 30 characters. In the Layout list, select a layout. Select a style from the Style drop-down list.

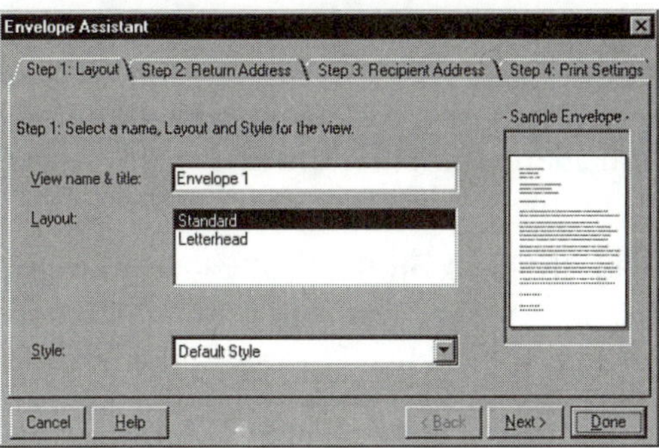

FIGURE 23.1 Select a layout for the envelopes.

3. Click the Next button. Approach displays Step 2, where you can type a return address.
4. If you want to include a return address on the envelope, type it in the Step 2 tab. Then click the Next button. If your envelopes already have a return address, simply click the Next button. Approach displays Step 3 of the Envelope Assistant (see Figure 23.2).

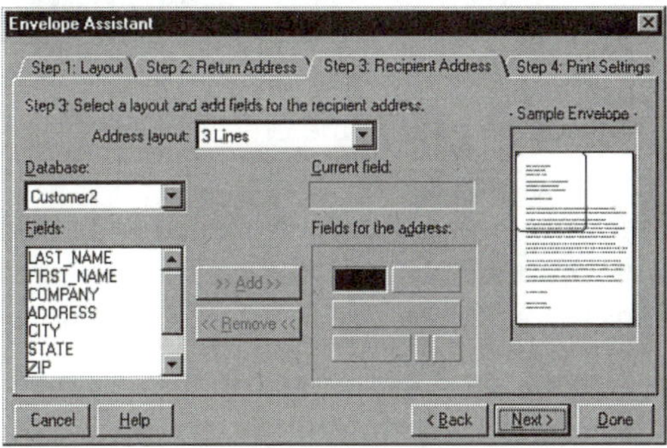

FIGURE 23.2 Select the layout for the address and add the fields.

5. To select the layout (number of address lines), display the Address layout drop-down list and select the one you want. Notice that Approach displays blanks for each area of a typical address and that the first area is selected in the Fields for the Address list.

6. In the Fields list, click on the field you want to include in the first address slot. Then click the Add button. Approach adds the field and moves to the next slot. Do this for each slot in the address.

7. When you are finished adding fields, click on the Next button. Approach displays Step 4 (see Figure 23.3).

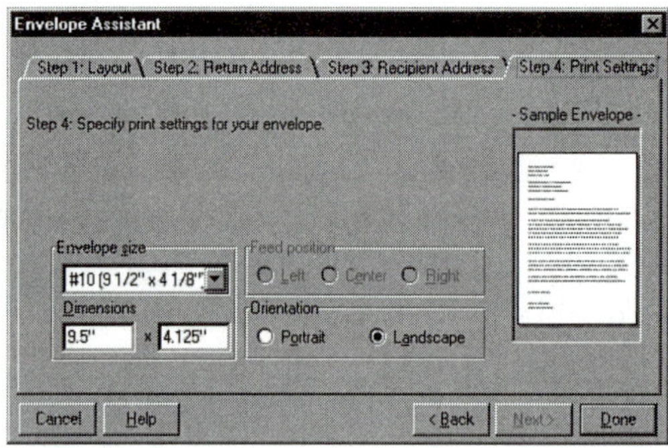

FIGURE 23.3 Select the size for the envelope.

8. Display the Envelope size drop-down list and select the size of envelope that you use. You can also enter the dimensions if you have a size that isn't listed.

9. Select an orientation. Landscape prints down the long edge of the envelope; portrait prints across.

10. Click the Done button. Approach creates the envelopes. You can use the File Print command to print this view.

CREATING MAILING LABELS

In addition to envelopes, you can also create mailing labels. Suppose that your form letter was one you mail out with your catalogs, and you need to use a big manila envelope for the catalog. Instead of setting up envelopes, you can create mailing labels. As another example, you may not even create a form letter, but instead may just need mailing labels—for instance, if you are mailing a package that doesn't require a letter.

My labels don't work on my printer! Keep in mind that your printer must be able to print on labels. Be sure to buy the type of label that your printer can use.

SETTING UP THE LABELS

To help you set up labels, Approach includes a Mailing Label Assistant that leads you step by step through the process. You simply need to know the type of label that you have. Follow these steps:

1. Open the Create menu and select the Mailing Label command. Approach displays the Mailing Label Assistant dialog box (see Figure 23.4).
2. In the Mailing label name text box, type a name for this view. The name will appear at the top of the Mailing Label tab.
3. Display the Label type drop-down list and select the type of label you are using.

Avery labels Avery is a popular label maker, so Approach enables you to select from one of many different Avery label products. If you buy a different type of label, check the package. Usually, the package will list the comparable Avery product.

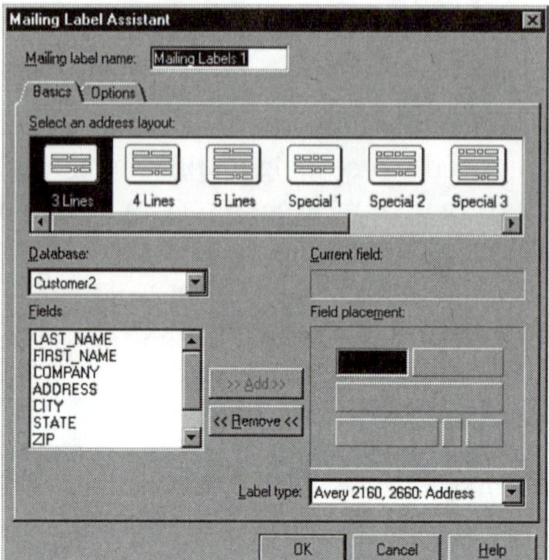

FIGURE 23.4 Select the layout and then add the fields using this dialog box.

4. In the Select an address layout area, select the layout that matches the labels you have. Notice that the Field placement area displays slots for the different lines and areas in a standard address. The first slot is selected.

5. In the Fields list, select the first field for the address and then click the Add button. Approach adds the field to the address label and moves to the next slot.

6. Continue to select fields and add them to the label until the address is complete.

7. Click the OK button. Approach creates the labels (see Figure 23.5).

Keep in mind that mailing labels are like any other view in Approach (such as a form or report). You can rearrange the fields, add text to the labels, change the formatting and more. See Lessons 16 and 17 for information on formatting a view.

You can also use the labels to enter data. Switch to Browse view; then you can make editing changes, if necessary, to any of the data.

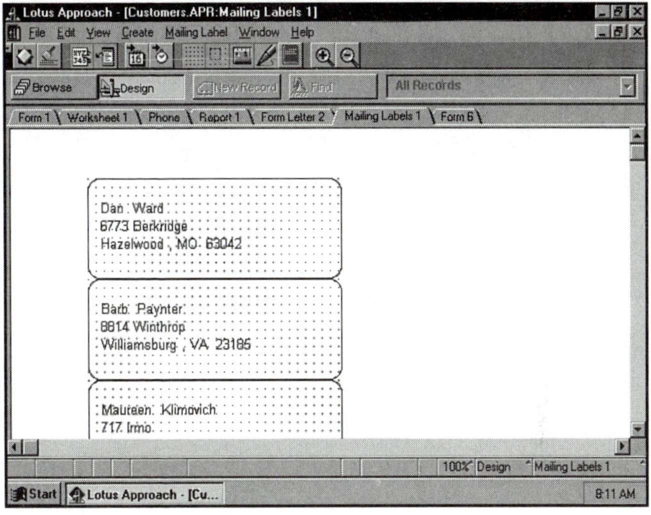

FIGURE 23.5 A sheet of labels.

PRINTING THE LABELS

Once the labels are set up just how you want, you can print them. Start by checking the overall view in Preview. Open the File menu and select the Print Preview command. If the labels look acceptable, you can print them.

Print labels for only some records If you want to print labels for only some of the records in the database, create a find request first. Also, if you want to keep the records in a specific order, sort before you create the labels.

To print the labels, follow these steps:

1. Insert the labels into the printer.
2. Open the File menu and select the Print command.
3. Click the OK button.

Which way do the labels go? If you are not sure which side of the paper the printer prints on, try this test. Put an X on the top of a piece of paper, put the piece of paper in with the X on top, and then print something. Check the printout to see where the X appears. If it appears on the same side as the print, put the labels in facing up. If it appears on the opposite side, put the labels in facing down.

In this lesson you learned how to create mailing labels and envelopes for your form letters. The next lesson covers how to work with another view of the database—a worksheet.

Creating a Worksheet

In this lesson, you'll learn how to work with data in a different view—a worksheet.

What Is a Worksheet?

When you set up a new database, Approach creates a new worksheet (a different view of the data). You can switch to this view to see how a worksheet is structured by clicking on the Worksheet tab.

If you have ever used a spreadsheet program such as Lotus 1-2-3, you are probably familiar with the concept of a worksheet. In this layout, you find a grid of columns and rows in which you can enter data. In an Approach worksheet, each column is a field, and each row is a record (see Figure 24.1). The intersection of a column and row is called a *cell*. The field names appear at the top of each column.

Entering and Editing Data in a Worksheet

If you prefer, you can use the worksheet to enter data. Some users may want to see more than one record at a time or may find it easier to move from record to record in the worksheet.

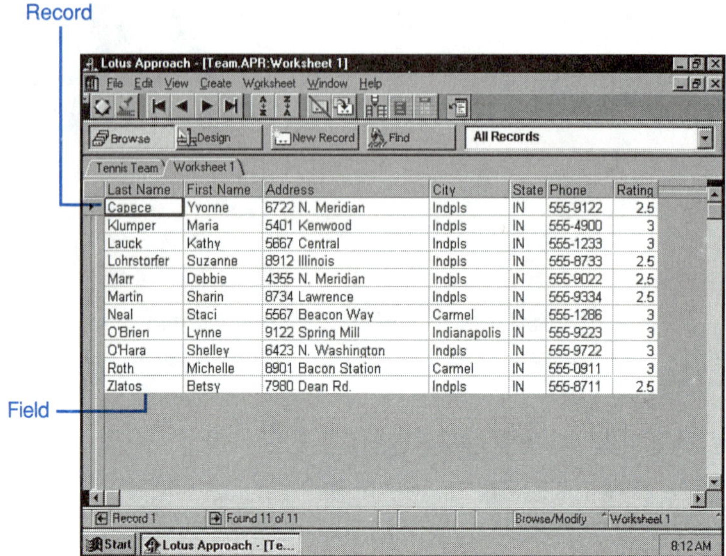

Last Name	First Name	Address	City	State	Phone	Rating
Capece	Yvonne	6722 N. Meridian	Indpls	IN	555-9122	2.5
Klumper	Maria	5401 Kenwood	Indpls	IN	555-4900	3
Lauck	Kathy	5667 Central	Indpls	IN	555-1233	3
Lohrstorfer	Suzanne	8912 Illinois	Indpls	IN	555-8733	2.5
Marr	Debbie	4355 N. Meridian	Indpls	IN	555-9022	2.5
Martin	Sharin	8734 Lawrence	Indpls	IN	555-9334	2.5
Neal	Staci	5567 Beacon Way	Carmel	IN	555-1286	3
O'Brien	Lynne	9122 Spring Mill	Indianapolis	IN	555-9223	3
O'Hara	Shelley	6423 N. Washington	Indpls	IN	555-9722	3
Roth	Michelle	8901 Bacon Station	Carmel	IN	555-0911	3
Zlatos	Betsy	7980 Dean Rd.	Indpls	IN	555-8711	2.5

FIGURE 24.1 In a worksheet, the data is arranged in columns (called records) and rows (or fields).

To enter data, be sure you are in Browse view. Then simply click in the record and field you want and then type the entry. You can press Tab to move from field to field. Press Shift+Tab to move backward through the fields. To move to the next record, you can use ↑ or ↓. Press Ctrl+N to add a new record.

You can also use the worksheet to edit data. Again, start in Browse view and then select the entry you want to change. Make the change and then move to another field or record.

Finally, you can use the Find and Sort commands in this view as well. (Open the Worksheet menu to find these commands.) Finding and sorting are covered in Lessons 10 and 11.

FORMATTING A WORKSHEET

Just like you can change the appearance of a form, you can also change how a worksheet appears. For example, you may want to make the columns wider. Or you may want to change the appearance of the field names so that they stand out more. Here is a list of how to make some of the most commonly made changes:

- To resize a column, put the pointer on the right border of the column you want to change. The pointer should display as a two-headed arrow (see Figure 24.2). Drag the column to resize.

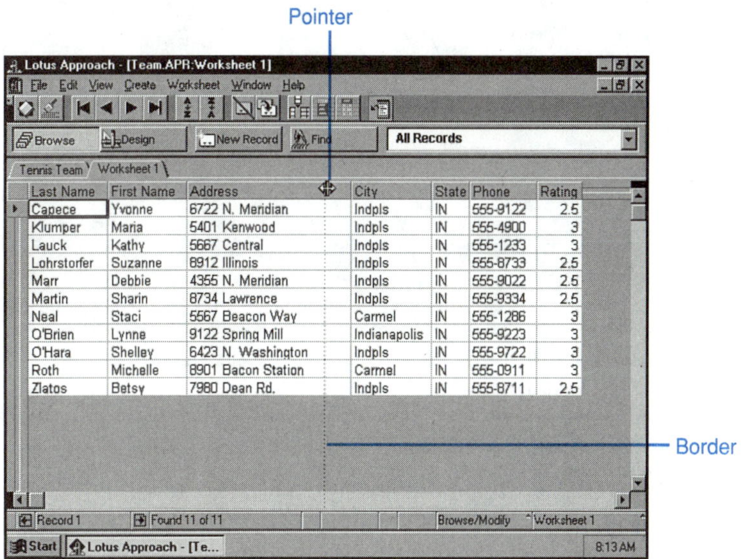

FIGURE 24.2 As you drag, you see an outline of the column border.

- To resize a row, put the pointer on the bottom border of the row and then drag to resize.

- To change the orders of the fields, select the field you want to move. Remember that fields are displayed as columns in a worksheet. You can select an entire column by clicking the column heading (see Figure 24.3). To move the field, drag the selected column to the place you want.

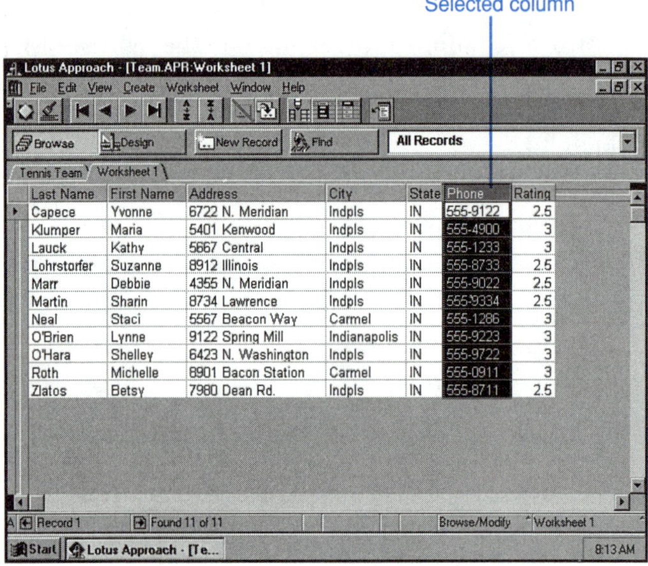

FIGURE 24.3 Select a column by clicking the column heading.

- To change the field names that appear as column headings, triple-click the headings. Then edit the heading or delete and type a new heading. You can also use the Worksheet, Edit Column Label command.

- To format the column headings, select a heading. Notice that the status bar includes buttons for changing the font (see Figure 24.4). You can use these buttons to select a font, size, style, text color, and alignment for the headings.

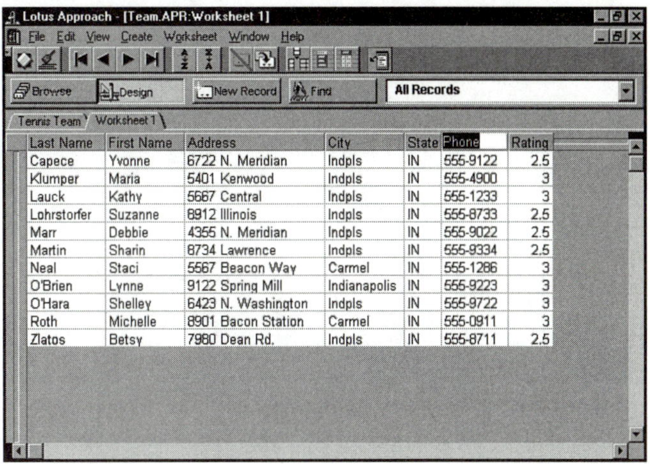

Figure 24.4 Use the status bar to format the headings.

Creating a New Worksheet

If you don't like the default worksheet that is set up, you can create a new one using the Worksheet Assistant. In the new worksheet, you can select the fields to include and the order in which to include them. Follow these steps to set up a new worksheet:

1. Open the Create menu and select the Worksheet command. Approach displays the Worksheet Assistant dialog box (see Figure 24.5).
2. In the Fields list, select the first field you want to include and click the Add button.
3. Continue to select fields and click the Add button until you add all the fields you want to include.
4. Click the Done button. Approach creates the worksheet.

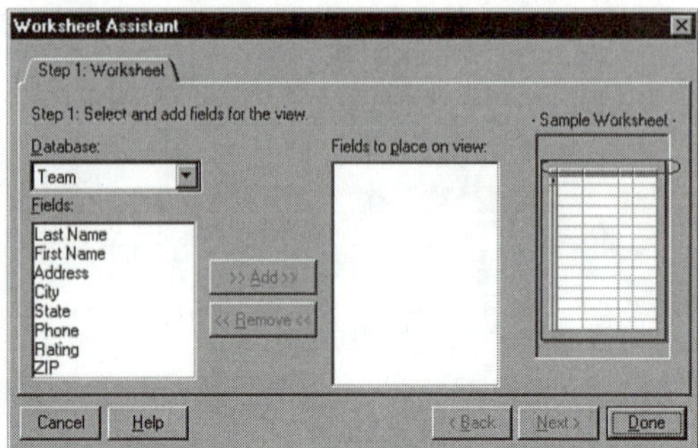

FIGURE 24.5 Use this tab to set up a new worksheet.

In this lesson you learned how to work with your data in a worksheet view. The next lesson explains how to use a special type of worksheet called a crosstab.

Creating a Crosstab

In this lesson, you will learn how to create a special type of worksheet called a crosstab.

What Is a Crosstab?

A crosstab is a worksheet that you can use to categorize and summarize the records in your database. Let's say that you have a database that tracks sales of your products by store. You could view a long list of sales and then try to get an idea of the overall performance of each product at each store. Or you could summarize the product sales using a crosstab, as illustrated in Figure 25.1.

Product Sales | Worksheet 1 | Crosstab 1 | Crosstab 2 | Chart 1 | Chart 2

	Indy Racquet Qty Sold	Racquet Man Qty Sold	Sports Center Qty Sold	*Total* Qty Sold
Big Bang	2	3		5
Blast		5		5
Force		4	4	8
Sledgehammer 4.8	12	12	12	36
Sledgehammer 5		4		4
Sledgehammer 6.2	1	6	7	14
Thunder	3	8	5	16
Total	18	42	28	88

Figure 25.1 A crosstab enables you to summarize data.

In this simple crosstab example, you can see both the quantity sold of each product (look across the rows) and the quantity sold by store (look down the columns). This summary information enables you to find out quite a lot about sales in one glance.

CREATING A CROSSTAB

Like most other types of views, Approach includes a Crosstab Assistant to lead you step by step through the process of creating this type of worksheet. Figure 25.2 shows the worksheet used for the crosstab in Figure 25.1. When you create a crosstab, you will be prompted to select the following:

Product Sales / Worksheet 1 / Crosstab 1 / Crosstab 2 / Chart 1 / Chart 2

Manufacturer	Racquet	Price	Store	Qty Sold
Wilson	Sledgehammer 4.8	229.99	Racquet Man	12
Wilson	Sledgehammer 6.2	189.99	Racquet Man	6
Wilson	Sledgehammer 5	139.99	Racquet Man	4
Prince	Thunder	179.99	Racquet Man	8
Prince	Blast	129.99	Racquet Man	5
Prince	Force	109.99	Racquet Man	4
Head	Big Bang	199.99	Racquet Man	3
Wilson	Sledgehammer 6.2	189.99	Sports Center	7
Wilson	Sledgehammer 4.8	229.99	Sports Center	12
Wilson	Sledgehammer 4.8	229.99	Indy Racquet	12
Wilson	Sledgehammer 6.2	189.99	Indy Racquet	1
Head	Big Bang	199.99	Indy Racquet	2
Prince	Force	109.99	Sports Center	4
Prince	Thunder	179.99	Sports Center	5
Prince	Thunder	179.99	Indy Racquet	3

FIGURE 25.2 This is the worksheet used to create the crosstab shown in the example.

Rows The field you select will be used as the first column in the crosstab. This is the data that you want to summarize. In the example in Figure 25.1, the Racquet field is selected for this step.

Columns The field(s) you select for columns will be used as the summary data in the crosstab (the remaining columns). You can select more than one column to use. In the example in Figure 25.1, the Store field is used for the columns.

Values As the third step in the Crosstab Assistant, you select the field you want to calculate. In the example in Figure 25.1, the Qty Sold field is used as the calculation field.

Follow these steps to create a crosstab:

1. Open the Create menu and select the Crosstab command. Approach displays the Step 1: Rows tab of the Crosstab Assistant dialog box (see Figure 25.3).

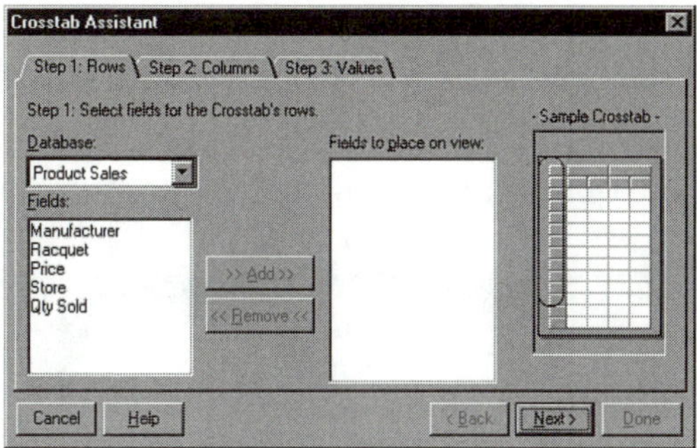

FIGURE 25.3 Select the rows to include in the crosstab.

2. Select the fields you want to include by clicking on the field and then clicking the Add button. These fields will be the rows in your crosstab.
3. Click the Next button. Approach displays the Step 2: Columns tab of the Crosstab Assistant dialog box (see Figure 25.4).

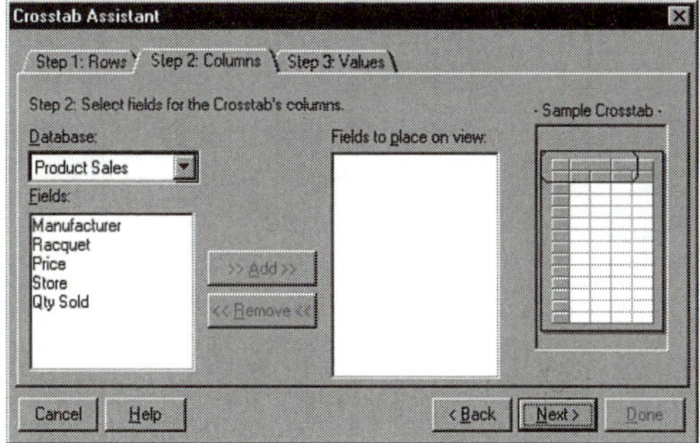

FIGURE 25.4 Select the columns to include in the crosstab.

4. In the Fields list, select the field(s) to include and then click the Add button. These fields will be included as columns in the crosstab.
5. Click the Next button. Approach displays the Step 3: Values of the Crosstab Assistant dialog box (see Figure 25.5).
6. Select the calculation you want performed and then the field to calculate.
7. Click the Done button. Approach creates the crosstab.

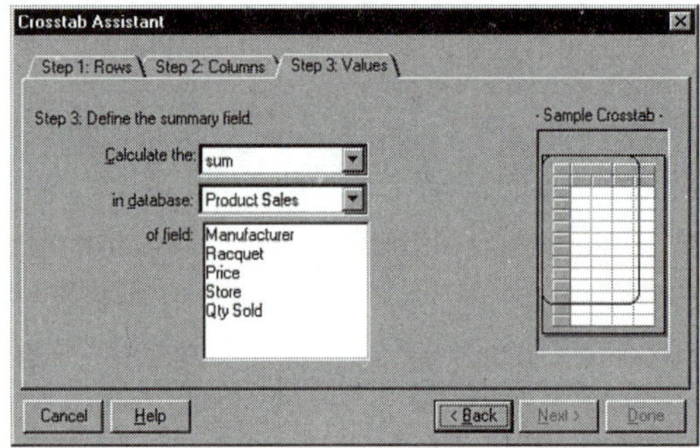

FIGURE 25.5 For this step, you can set up the calculation to perform.

You can use any of the worksheet editing and formatting skills on this crosstab that you learned in Lesson 24. You can also print the view by opening the File menu and selecting the Print command.

In this lesson you learned how to create a crosstab worksheet. The next lesson discusses charts, another type of view that can help you visually summarize data.

Creating a Chart

LESSON 26

In this lesson, you will learn how to chart your data using one of several different chart types.

What Is a Chart?

A *chart* takes your numeric data and represents that information visually. As the old saying goes, "A picture is worth a thousand words." Charts not only visually represent the data, but they can sometimes help you more easily spot trends and patterns. For example, if you create a pie chart of sales by region, you can quickly see which of the regions has the greatest sales by seeing which has the biggest "slice" of the pie.

Chart A chart represents your numeric data visually. Table 26.1 lists some typical chart styles.

A chart consists of different elements, identified in Figure 26.1. Each data point is plotted along the y-axis (here the data points are the individual products, indicated in the legend). You can plot more than one set of data points, called *series*. In this figure, the series are the stores.

Series In a chart, more than one set of data points is called a series.

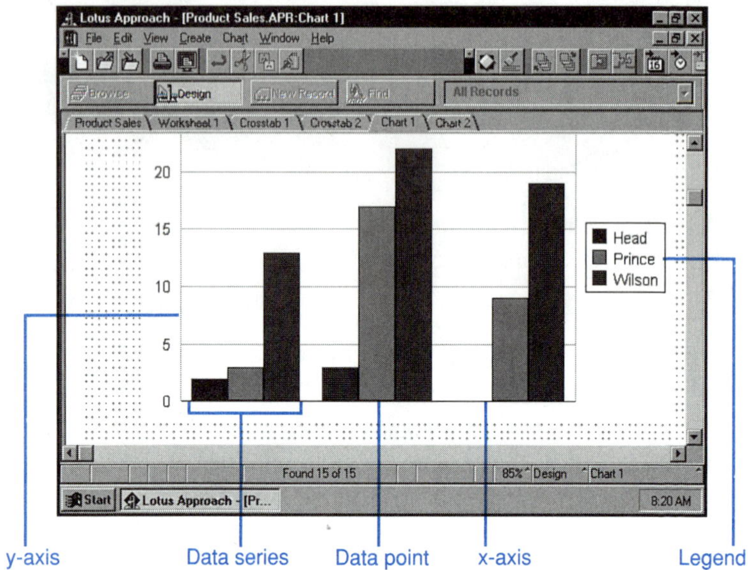

FIGURE 26.1 Approach enables you to represent your data visually.

You can use Approach to create one of several different types of charts.

UNDERSTANDING CHART TYPES

Before you start creating a chart, you should be familiar with the different chart types (described in Table 26.1). Doing so will help you select the correct chart type for your message.

TABLE 26.1 DIFFERENT CHART TYPES

CHART TYPE	DESCRIPTION
Bar	The data in this type of chart are graphed as vertical bars (like a column). If you want to compare individual data points, this type of chart works well.

CHART TYPE	DESCRIPTION
Line	The data in this type of chart are plotted as points and the points are connected with a line. Use this type of chart to show trends.
Area	Use this type of data to compare relationships. Each data point is charted on a line and the area beneath the line is colored in.
Pie	Data in this type of chart is plotted as a slice of the pie. Use this type of chart to show the relationship of one data point to the whole.

The rest of this lesson describes how to create these chart types.

CREATING A BAR, LINE, OR AREA CHART

Bar, line, and area charts look different but are created the same way. For these chart types, you can plot more than one series.

To help you create a chart, Approach includes the Chart Assistant, with four basic steps. Simply follow these steps to get started:

1. Open the Create menu and select the Chart command. Approach displays the Chart Assistant, with the Step 1: Layout tab selected (see Figure 26.2).
2. In the View name & title text box, type a name for the chart. This name is used as the title and on the View tab. You can type up to 30 characters.

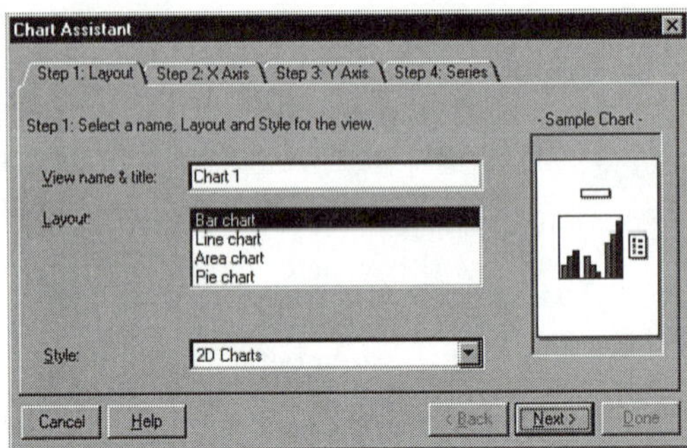

FIGURE 26.2 The Chart Assistant, with the Step 1 tab selected.

3. Select the type of chart you want in the Layout list.
4. Select a style (2D or 3D) from the Style drop-down list.
5. Click the Next button. Approach displays the Step 2: X Axis tab (see Figure 26.3).

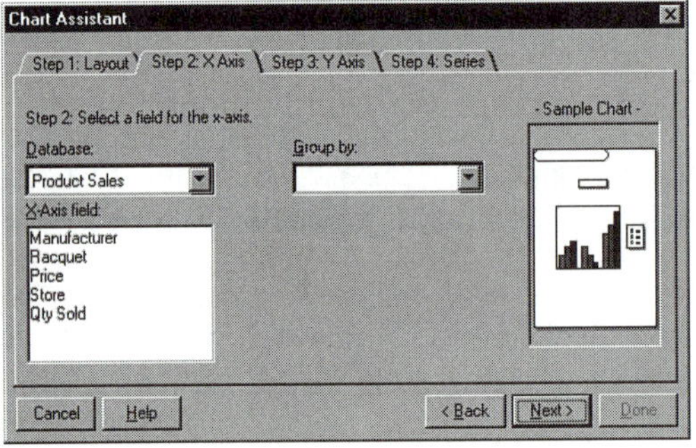

FIGURE 26.3 Select the field to use for the x-axis.

6. Select the field you want to use as the x-axis. This is the field that will be plotted along the x-axis.
7. Click the Next button. Approach displays the Step 3: Y Axis tab (see Figure 26.4).

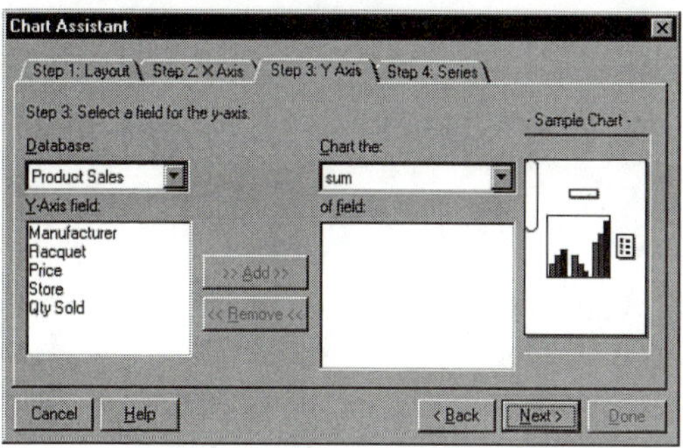

FIGURE 26.4 Select the calculation for the y-axis.

8. Select the calculation to perform and then select the field to calculate. For instance, to chart the total units sold, you would select sum as the function and Qty Sold as the field.
9. Click the Next button. Approach displays the Step 4: Series tab (see Figure 26.5).

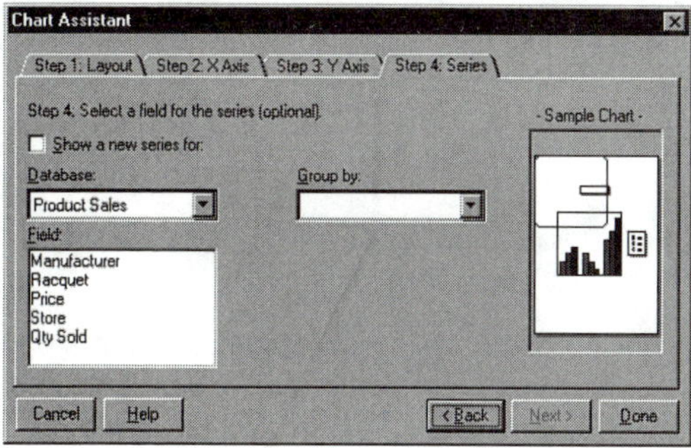

FIGURE 26.5 The Step 4 tab enables you to select the series.

10. If you want to chart more than one series, select the field to group as the series from the Field list. To group the series by store, for example, select the Store field here.
11. Click the Done button. Approach creates the chart.

You can make design changes (for example, adding or formatting a chart title) by switching to Design view. For more on this, see Lesson 12. To print the chart, use the File Print command.

Creating a Pie Chart

In a pie chart, you chart only one set of data points, and each is represented as a slice of pie. You can use the Chart Assistant to create this type of chart, but you need to complete only two tabs. The first tab is the same as that for the bar, line, and area chart. You can follow steps 1–5 in the preceding section to complete this tab.

For the Step 2 tab, you select a field for each pie wedge, a calculation, and a field to be calculated (see Figure 26.6). Approach then creates the pie chart.

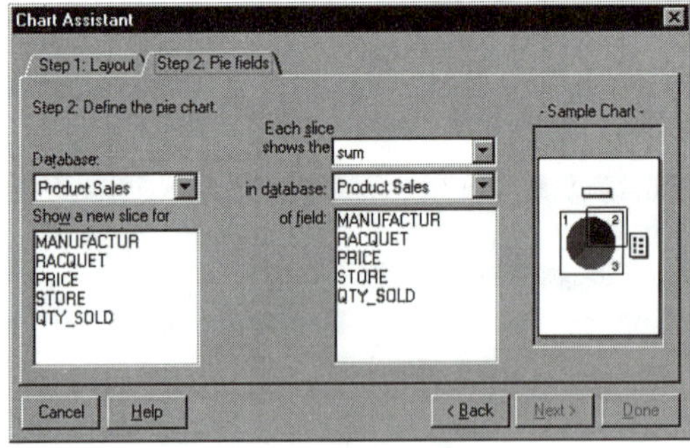

Figure 26.6 Pie charts are less complex and therefore easier to create.

Save the Approach file A chart is just another view. To save the chart, you need to save the Approach file using the Save Approach File command in the File menu.

In this lesson you learned how to create a chart. The next lesson covers how to work with more than one database.

Joining Databases

LESSON 27

In this lesson, you will learn how to work with more than one database.

What Is a Join?

If you had to keep all your data in one database, that database would soon become unwieldy. For instance, consider a database for a small business. If you kept track of your customers, products, orders, and inventory all in one database, how would you ever get it set up efficiently? How would you handle all that information?

Instead, you can create several databases and *join* them when you want to share data among them. For example, you can keep your customers in one database and your orders in another. When you want to match customers to orders, you can join the two databases and then create a report. You could also have a separate database for your products that you could link to your order database. You can create any type of view using data from more than one database.

Join When you work with more than one database, and those databases share data among themselves, you *join* the databases.

Relational database Approach is a *relational* database, which means you can use data from more than one database. In the opposite type of database, *flat file*, you can use only data in that one database.

SETTING UP A JOINED DATABASE

You can't just take two databases and join them unless you do a little planning beforehand. To join a database, you have to connect them—establish the relationship between the two sets of data. You do this by including one (or more) fields that are the same in both databases. The field(s) you select must uniquely identify the record. For instance, in a customer database, you can't use the last name field because you may have more than one customer with the same last name. Most often you include some type of ID field.

To link the orders to a customer, you can also include a customer ID field in the orders database. This field, called the *join field*, is the connection between the two databases. With this field, Approach can match the records from the different databases.

When you set up the relationships, you can have a one-to-many relationship or a many-to-one relationship. For instance, the customer could have more than one order, so that relationship would be a one-to-many relationship. If you included a product number in your product database and in your order database, you would have the reverse type of relationship; the orders for a product (many) would refer to the specific product (one) in the product database. You can also set up many-to-many relationships, but that type of join is beyond the scope of this book.

JOINING A DATABASE

When you want to work with data from more than one database, you can create a join. You can then create a form, report, or other view using data from the joined databases.

Follow these steps to join a database:

1. Open the database that you want to start with. This database contains the records and fields you want to join with another database.

2. Open the Create menu and select the Join command. Approach displays the Join dialog box (see Figure 27.1). In this dialog box, the fields in the current database are listed.

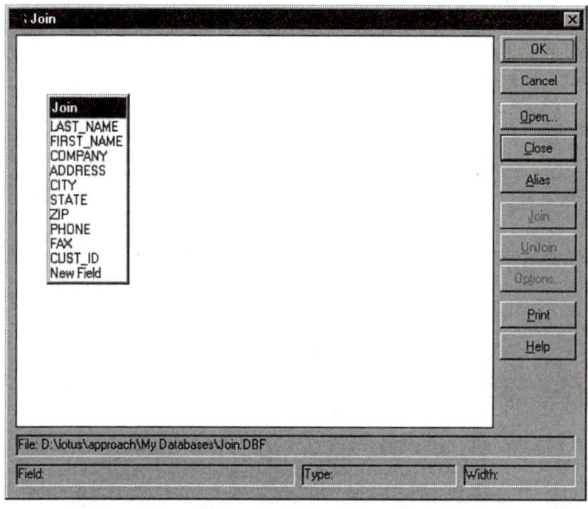

FIGURE 27.1 The Join dialog box lists the fields in the open database.

3. Click the Open button to display the Open dialog box.
4. Open the database that you want to join. For information on opening a database file, see Lesson 7. When you open the database, the fields for that database are displayed in the Join dialog box.
5. To join a field, click on the field and then drag it to the join field in the other database. You can also click the first field, click the join field, and then click the Join button. The two databases are connected with a line showing the join (see Figure 27.2).
6. Click the OK button. Approach joins the databases.

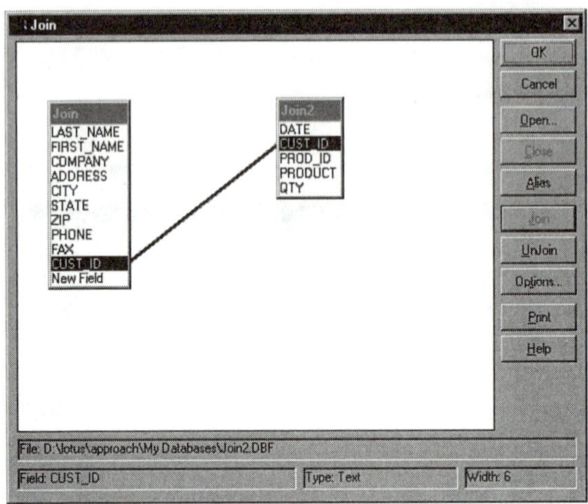

FIGURE 27.2 A line indicates the join.

Field not valid? You can't use just any field for the join; the field must uniquely identify the record. Most of the time, an ID field works best as the join field.

WORKING WITH JOINED DATABASES

Once the databases are joined, you can use data in either of the databases in a report, form, or other view. Previous lessons in this book described how to create these different views. When working with multiple databases, keep these concepts in mind:

- When you are selecting the fields for the view, you can select a different database by displaying the Database drop-down list. Select the database you want, and then Approach will display the available fields in the Fields list. You can add fields from the different databases, as shown in Figure 27.3. Creating forms is covered in Lesson 18, creating reports in Lesson 19.

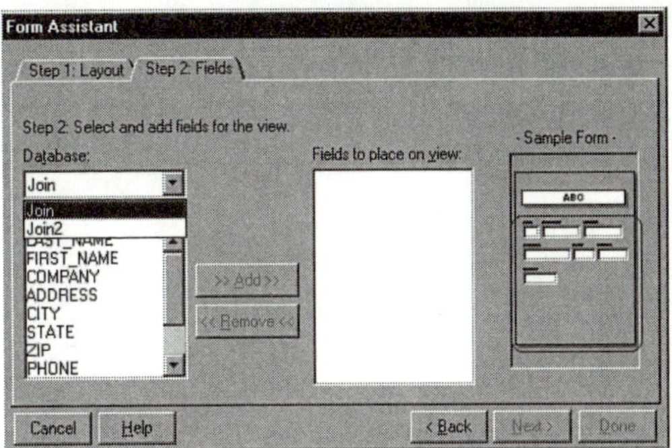

FIGURE 27.3 Display the Database drop-down list to select a different database.

- When you create a view, you have to specify the main database—that is, the database in which you want all records to appear. When you create a view, you are prompted to define the main database (see Figure 27.4). Each record in the main database will have its one page in the view.

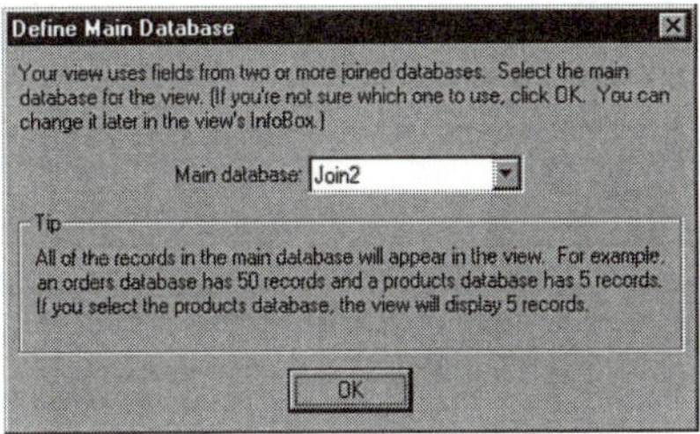

FIGURE 27.4 The Define Main Database dialog box.

- The joined database or detail database will provide additional information or supporting data for the view. The matching data from the detail database is presented in a repeating panel.

Detail database The database that provides additional or supporting data.

Repeating panel A part of a form or report that shows data from detail records that are related to the main record.

UNJOINING A DATABASE

If you don't need the join any longer, you can unjoin the two databases. Follow these steps:

1. Open the Create menu and select the Join command. You see the Join dialog box.
2. Click the line that joins the two databases. Then click the Unjoin button.
3. Click the OK button.

In this lesson you learned how to work with data from more than one database.

INDEX

C

D

G-H

I

J-K

L

M

N

O

P-Q

R

S

T

U-V

W

X-Y-Z

Complete and Return this Card for a *FREE* Computer Book Catalog

Thank you for purchasing this book! You have purchased a superior computer book written expressly for your needs. To continue to provide the kind of up-to-date, pertinent coverage you've come to expect from us, we need to hear from you. Please take a minute to complete and return this self-addressed, postage-paid form. In return, we'll send you a free catalog of all our computer books on topics ranging from word processing to programming and the internet.

:. ☐ Mrs. ☐ Ms. ☐ Dr. ☐

ıme (first) ☐☐☐☐☐☐☐☐☐☐☐ (M.I.) ☐ (last) ☐☐☐☐☐☐☐☐☐☐☐☐☐☐☐

ldress ☐☐☐☐☐☐☐☐☐☐☐☐☐☐☐☐☐☐☐☐☐☐☐☐☐☐☐☐☐☐☐☐☐☐☐

☐☐☐☐☐☐☐☐☐☐☐☐☐☐☐☐☐☐☐☐☐☐☐☐☐☐☐☐☐☐☐☐☐☐☐

ty ☐☐☐☐☐☐☐☐☐☐☐☐☐☐☐ State ☐☐ Zip ☐☐☐☐☐ ☐☐☐☐☐

one ☐☐☐ ☐☐☐ ☐☐☐☐ Fax ☐☐☐ ☐☐☐ ☐☐☐☐

mpany Name ☐☐☐☐☐☐☐☐☐☐☐☐☐☐☐☐☐☐☐☐☐☐☐☐☐☐☐☐☐☐☐☐

mail address ☐☐☐☐☐☐☐☐☐☐☐☐☐☐☐☐☐☐☐☐☐☐☐☐☐☐☐☐☐☐☐☐

. Please check at least (3) influencing factors for purchasing this book.

- ront or back cover information on book .... ☐
- pecial approach to the content .... ☐
- ompleteness of content .... ☐
- uthor's reputation .... ☐
- ublisher's reputation .... ☐
- ook cover design or layout .... ☐
- ıdex or table of contents of book .... ☐
- rice of book .... ☐
- pecial effects, graphics, illustrations .... ☐
- ther (Please specify): __________ ☐

:. How did you first learn about this book?

- ıternet Site .... ☐
- aw in Macmillan Computer Publishing catalog .... ☐
- ecommended by store personnel .... ☐
- aw the book on bookshelf at store .... ☐
- ecommended by a friend .... ☐
- eceived advertisement in the mail .... ☐
- aw an advertisement in: __________ ☐
- ead book review in: __________ ☐
- ther (Please specify): __________ ☐

. How many computer books have you purchased in the last six months?

his book only .... ☐ 3 to 5 books .... ☐
books .... ☐ More than 5 .... ☐

4. Where did you purchase this book?

- Bookstore .... ☐
- Computer Store .... ☐
- Consumer Electronics Store .... ☐
- Department Store .... ☐
- Office Club .... ☐
- Warehouse Club .... ☐
- Mail Order .... ☐
- Direct from Publisher .... ☐
- Internet site .... ☐
- Other (Please specify): .... ☐

5. How long have you been using a computer?

Less than 6 months .. ☐ 6 months to a year ..... ☐
1 to 3 years .... ☐ More than 3 years ...... ☐

6. What is your level of experience with personal computers and with the subject of this book?

	With PC's	With subject of book
New	☐	☐
Casual	☐	☐
Accomplished	☐	☐
Expert	☐	☐

Source Code — ISBN: 0-7897-0647-4

7. Which of the following best describes your job title?

- Administrative Assistant ☐
- Coordinator ☐
- Manager/Supervisor ☐
- Director ☐
- Vice President ☐
- President/CEO/COO ☐
- Lawyer/Doctor/Medical Professional ☐
- Teacher/Educator/Trainer ☐
- Engineer/Technician ☐
- Consultant ☐
- Not employed/Student/Retired ☐
- Other (Please specify): ☐

8. Which of the following best describes the area of the company your job title falls under?

- Accounting ☐
- Engineering ☐
- Manufacturing ☐
- Marketing ☐
- Operations ☐
- Sales ☐
- Other (Please specify): ☐

9. What is your age?

- Under 20 ☐
- 21-29 ☐
- 30-39 ☐
- 40-49 ☐
- 50-59 ☐
- 60-over ☐

10. Are you:

- Male ☐
- Female ☐

11. Which computer publications do you read regularly? (Please list)

____

____

____

____

____

____

____

____

____

Comments: ______________________________

____

____

Fold here and scotch-tape to

NO POSTAGE NECESSARY IF MAILED IN THE UNITED STATES

BUSINESS REPLY MAIL

FIRST-CLASS MAIL PERMIT NO. 9918 INDIANAPOLIS IN

POSTAGE WILL BE PAID BY THE ADDRESSEE

ATTN MARKETING
MACMILLAN COMPUTER PUBLISHING
MACMILLAN PUBLISHING USA
201 W 103RD ST
INDIANAPOLIS IN 46209-9042